The Blackman's Stolen Birthright

Stolen Knowledge of God

The Blackman's Stolen Birthright

Stolen Knowledge of God

ALFRED ALI

Published by
Alfred Ali Literary Works
P.O. Box 27206
Detroit, Mi. 48227

FIRST EDITION

All rights reserved, including the right of
reproduction in whole or in any part in any form.

Copyright 1992 by Alfred Ali

Published by Alfred Ali Literary Works
P.O. Box 27206, Detroit, MI 48227

Manufactured in the United States of America
ISBN: 0-963-60250-0

Library of Congress Catalog Card No: 93-70400

Distributor:

BOOKWORLD, Services, Inc.
1933 Whitfield Loop
Sarasota, FL 34243
1-800-444-2524 ext 253

DEDICATION

This book is dedicated to my wife Martha, son James Alfred, daughter Joanna, and the rest of my family; especially my mother Mrs. Louise Johnson. A special thanks to Hon. Elijah Muhammad for his courage, steadfastness, dedication to duty, and love of this work of raising the dead (Spiritually) back to life. Thank you Dear Holy Apostle! A Special Thanks to Retired-Chief Harold Watkins for his understanding of me and this work.

TABLE OF CONTENTS

Preface: Blackman, Know Thyself;
THE BLACKMAN IS THE SUPREME BEING!   xi

Introduction: The War of Armageddon is a war within yourself   xv

Chapter I. Abraham: Children of Israel (History of Black People in Scripture)   1

Chapter II. Moses, The Ten Commandments   9
     A. Adam and Eve and this Children of Israel are White people   9
     B. Children of Israel (white people) exiled into the caves   10
     C. Moses sent to reform White people   11

Chapter III. The "Life" of Jesus Christ (Physical Birth, Spiritual Birth, Ministry, Crucifiction and Resurrection)   15
     A. Birth of Jesus (Mary and Joseph) (Spiritual Birth)   19
     B. Birth of Jesus and his Ministry (Resurrection of The Dead)!   23
     C. Crucifiction and Resurrection of Jesus!   26

Chapter IV. Whiteman's Tricknology was the beginning of the Blackman's Stolen Birthright In America   34
     A. Islam is Man's true Religion   36
     B. Gold is just lying of the ground in America (A Trick)   37
     C. The Making of A Negro   38
     D. History repeats Itself; Blacks exiled in America (Cave)   39

CONTENTS

Chapter V. Master Fard Muhammad is the God that came to Restore the Blackman's Birthright		42
A.	History of Master Fard Muhammad	42
B.	World Traveler	44
C.	Reality of God and the Devil	45
Chapter VI. The First Jesus Christ		54
A.	Ibin Yusef	54
B.	Jesus (IBin Yusef) taught Love Thy Neighbor as Thyself	55
Chapter VII. The Dwellers In The Cave		61
A.	A Lost People for 375 years	61
B.	Whiteman was made to rule through tricks and not Truth; 6,000 years	63
C.	Gog and Magog describes their history; Holy Quran Chapter 18 v94	66
D.	Cain and Abel; Bible Genesis 4: 1–2	68
Chapter VIII. Behold I Send You Elijah To establish A New Moral-System and Economy for the Blackman)		70
A.	Negroes Identity will be restored	70
B.	The Laws of Islam and the Orthodox Jews Laws are similar	74
C.	Jesus and Necodemus	78
D.	The Stone (Blacks) that the builders (Whites) rejected	79
Chapter IX. The real History of Pharaoh and the Children of Israel		87
A.	Blackman's identity was stolen from him	87
B.	The Negro's mind was made dependent on the Whiteman's Economy	89
C.	Dred Scott Decision	91
D.	Slavery fashioned and shaped the Mind of the Blackman	91
Chapter X. Blacks are slaves today because of Law and Economics!		93
A.	1868 The Fourteenth Amendment (A trick)	93
B.	1955 Desegregation of the Schools (A trick)	94

C.	1964 Civil Rights Act prohibits Discrimination (A trick)	96
D.	Joseph (Blackman of USA) spiritually united with Asia and Africa	97
E.	The Children of Israel (Blacks Spiritual Identity) will be raised from the Dead	100
F.	White people have the world thinking that they are the real Children of Israel (Another trick)	103
G.	Joseph dream will be fulfilled in the United States	105
H.	The Blackman is living within the Seventh Thousand Year; A change in world powers from white to black; from wrong to right	113

Chapter XI. Blackman's Re-birth, must include the following Knowledge of Self 118

A.	Afrocentricity	118
B.	Separate Economics!	121
C.	History of Self	124
D.	His Own Religion	125
E.	His Own Culture	126
F.	His Own Name	128
G.	He must be re-born with the conception of his own God	129
H.	Blackman must understand who he is in scripture; Blackman's spiritual problem is in living a false belief in Christianity	131
I.	Misunderstanding about the Bible and Holy Quran	134
J.	Dead means a mental and spiritual state of mind	135

Chapter XII. The Blackman True Identity is Divine ... 141

A.	Creation of the Blackman	141
B.	Heaven and Hell is in this Life	144

Chapter XIII. Colonialism will be broken from the backs of Black People 149

A.	Colonialism is a Way of Life for White People	149
B.	The First Resurrection	151

x   CONTENTS

Chapter XIV. The Final War: Regaining the Blackman's Birthright, Economy and Moral System. Ye shall know the Truth and the Truth shall make you free John 8:32 "The knowledge of God and the Devil"   154

Conclusion: EVERY NATION (BLACK PEOPLE) MUST BUILD ON IT'S OWN BIRTHRIGHT; BECAUSE THAT IS A NATION'S FOUNDATION. *"The Final War will not be Nuclear, but rather a Race War. Genesis 27:40. to regain the Birthright.*   172

Reference: Correct Meaning of Scriptural Terms!   179
1. Heaven and Hell   179
2. Life After Death   180
3. Spiritual Law (How Man becomes Complete Within Himself)   181
4. The Problem   182
5. Material Civilization   183
6. Prophets of God   184
7. Misunderstanding About Bible   186
8. Jesus Meaning Of The Resurrection   187

Index   189

PREFACE:
Blackman, Know Thy-Self! Blackman Is The Supreme Being!

The purpose of this book is to show how the Whiteman gained control and authority over Black, Brown, Red, and Yellow Mankind. The number one issue of the nineties for the United States and the world is "Mental Instability due to Joblessness" and a change in the Economic power structure of the Whiteman. This will bring about conditions in many cultural and domestic ways that will rock the consciousness of the races, and bring about new crisis in race relations; i.e. Rodney King. The scriptures (Bible and Holy Quran) are the only source that provides an insight into the current condition; WATCH THE RACE RELATIONS IN THE USA!

The Civil Rights Bill is now called a "Quota Bill for Jobs" by President Bush. Whites are protesting Black Students for having a "Black Graduation" besides the normal or traditional "White Graduation". Prisons are sixty-five per cent black with young black males with no hope for the future. Is Religion Important? In the penal system of the United States, the only hope for some blacks is Islam. This is the Black Man true religion and it provides the knowledge that he was lacking before being sent to prison. That is the knowledge of Who He Is, the knowledge of Who Is God, Who Is the Devil, and most of all the knowledge of the time and what must be done.

Is Religion Important? The religion of Islam is the salvation of Black people the world over, because a world change or the Judgement of the world is taking place and most people know it not. The Religion of Islam has the answers. The average individual has been taught to think in terms of Economics for all his questions and answers about life; Black Economics is the solution to problems today. *The separation of the Black man from the way of life of the Whiteman is a Divine separation.* Economics and Religion must work together for the benefit of thepeo-ple however, this battle is between God and the Devil Spiritually.

It is God in the person of Master Fard Muhammad that is calling for separation, and it is the Religion of Islam as taught by the Hon. Elijah Muhammad that is sounding the trumpet. WAKE UP BLACKMAN TO YOUR Religion. SEPARATION IS THE KEY! Negroes are Dead to their own way of life. Before being "Made" Negroes in America, Black People lived a life of total Righteousness within their own nation. Allah means "All in All" or Submission to Righteousness as "A Way of Life." Devil means A People or Person that lives a life of Evil as "A Way of Life. Black People (Righteous) have lived under the Rule of Unrighteousness for 6,000 years, it is time to Separatate Mentally and Spiritually from this Lifestyle of Evil.

The foundation or base for this book is Man Know Thyself and is taken from the scriptures; Bible 1 Corinthians 3:16 Know Ye not that ye are the Temple of God, and that the Spirit of God dwelleth in you? Holy Quran Chapter 15, Section 3, Verse 26–29

26 And surely we created Man of sounding clay, of black mud fashioned into shape.
27 And the jinn, we created before of intensely hot fire.
28 And when thy Lord said to the angels: I am going to create a mortal of sounding clay, of black mud fashioned into shape.
29 So when I have made him complete and breathed into him my spirit, fall down making obesiance to him.

These two scriptures proves that God dwells within Man (Not in the sky) the first Man God made to rule and govern this earth was himself. God and the Blackman are One. For over four-hundred years, the Blackman has been "Captured Mentally" by lies, myths, and falsehood; it is now time Divinely that he be "Set-Free with the Truth!" John 8:32 Jesus said, Ye shall know the Truth, and the Truth shall make you free. The Blackman Is The Supreme Being!

However, the Truth will not Set the Blackman's mind free unless he proves it to himself in his own experience. He must demonstrate it, apply this truth daily in his life, live a righteous life, and he will come to know who God and the Devil really is; and thus bring about the Resurrection of the Dead as a fact of life! HE MUST ACCEPT HIS BIRTHRIGHT (Own Heritage).

The Blackman's True Identity!

The Blackman is the Original Man (first) of the planet earth, and he established the first civilization for human beings. In the last 6,000 years, every race of people have ruled the planet except him, it is now time to regain rulership of his home; the planet earth! The Blackman is the Cream of the nations and will rise to the top with his own Way of Life.

INTRODUCTION:
The War of Armageddon is a Mental War within Yourself

Armageddon means armies gathered together to do battle. It is referred to as the last great battle on earth between God and the Devil. It is the war to end all wars. However, many people of earth mis-understood the War of Armageddon and its battlefield. The war is a mental and spiritual war wherein the people of earth must decide to accept God's way of life (righteousness) or the Devil's way of life (unrighteousness), and the battlefield is the Mind of Man. This is the same condition that the world was in six-thousand years ago when Adam and Eve (white people) were expelled from the Garden of Eden for disobeying God's laws, only now it is the final Judgement, there is no more extension of time for people that reject God. This is what the War of Armageddon is all about.

During the extension of time that God gave to, Adam and Eve, or White people, they were allowed to roam the earth and contaminate the population with their way of life (lying, cheating, stealing, fornicating, robbery and murdering the people of the earth) until their time was up in 1914. Now, the world is going through a transition of power and a change in lifestyles. For six-thousand years, the world has been living under "Unrighteousness" and now the people are beginning to adjust to living under a righteous ruler (God) in the person of Fard Muhammad, the Supreme Being himself. Behold, I Make All thing New, Rev. 21:5!

The people of earth have not lived under righteousness for so long that they are unaccustomed to it or "Dead", so this period of time is called the Resurrection of the Dead, in order to wake the people up to what must be done. The devil is frantically trying to keep the people mentally and spiritually asleep to who he is; this battle of waking the people up or keeping them asleep to the knowledge of God and the Devil is known as the War of Armageddon. After the people wake up, then the Judgement will set in, and the power of the Devil to rule over the earth will be broken forever. The War of Armageddon is All In The Mind.

In the beginning, the blackman, the first Man, was ignorant as to his real identity (God). There were many things worshiped as God like the Sun, Moon, the heavens, rocks, and any thing else that fascinated his imagination. Snakes, bulls, cows, and other animals were bowned down and serves as God. This process was practiced through millions of years, and civilization after civilization. There were no other races on earth! The blackman is not a race but a Nation. In fact, the black nation is the only real nation on earth because all races evolved from his genes and a Race has a beginning and a end. The Blackman has no beginning (recorded beginning) nor does he have an ending; because the beginning and end starts with him.

The circumference of the earth is 24,896 miles or approximately 25,000 miles around the globe. Master Fard Muhammad (Supreme Being) said that the history of the blackman is written up every 25,000 years in advance, and when a portion of it is to be fulfilled, then that portion is extracted from the record books and given to a Man (Prophet or Messenger) and this Man relates this (Script of writing known as a Scripture) to the people that he was sent. He is not responsible whether the people adhere to the scripture or not. Now, this is the way Scripture or History is made.

When the past 25,000 year history is up, and it is time for a new history for the people to live by; the King or Ruler gathers all the Wise scientist, scholars, clergymen, and forecasters to go among the people that exist on earth wherever they may be, and record their thoughts about the future. All of these thoughts from the people are to scrutinized, analyzed, and projected into the future as to what was going to happen to the public. The people did not know and still don't know that it is "their own Thinking that determines their future". The people think that it is God that is doing these things, not knowing that they are the God that is doing it!

The War of Armegeddon is designed to get Man to stop this internal war within himself and accept himself for who he truly is, Self-Creator, He is the cause of his own Heaven or Hell.

The Revelator of the Bible tells you that certain portions of the book (Bible) is given in portions to the people by a Prophet. This is done to protect the works of the past period of history, and the new people will have to do their work on their own without the aid of a previous civilization knowledge. For example, this six-thousand year period does not know anything about the past period of seven-thousand years or so. What remains is the remnants of the blackman's civilization like the Pyramids and Sphinx. The period of history (The making of the Races) will culminate with Man being more more aware of himself than ever before in history. Which is the purpose of the whole ordeal (self-knowledge). Master Fard Muhammad teaches that they (Blackman) have searched the earth millions of years and now they have CONCLUDED, they have come to a DECISION, that there is no God on earth or above the earth, other than the Son of Man, the Blackman. All creativity, all life originated out of his being!

That is the purpose of this book, to show who the Blackman really is. The contents of the book deals with this six-thousand years period, wherein a new Man was made to rule over the blackman for a period of time, and God comes in the end and put to rest his rule by exposing him with the Truth. John 8:32 Know the Truth and the truth will make you free. Why is it that people use scripture to explain the truth? Because when the blackman gathers up the history of the people for their future, that Thinking of the people becomes their scripture or script of writing. It is put in a book, called Bible, (Bible only means a collection of writings) In fact, the Blackman is the originator of the Bible and Holy Quran. Everything that is happening today has been written down beforehand, nothing is a mystery to the blackman. But remember, the people have been put to sleep with falsehood and the reality of life is that one must wake up first, before this truth can make them free trough deeds and actions. In order to Wake-Up, you must Believe, then God within self will do the rest. Proverbs 23:7 As a Man Thinketh In his heart (Mind) So is he; Be he God or Devil!

This book revolves around the Bible's concept of Jacob stealing his brother Esau's blessing and birthright from him. This actually took place in America with the Whiteman stealing the Blackman's birthright in slavery. The Blackman of America is fighting his own War of Mental Armegeddon within his Mind. He is deciding whether to Build his Birthright and follows God once again or remain in the condition that he is in at present (A mental and Spiritual Slave) to the Whiteman's birthright and Money System.

A Divine Secret

The true knowledge of Who God Is, and Who the Devil Is, was kept as a Secret FROM THE GENERAL PUBLIC, until the end of this age; Which in Now! read Matthews 13:24:43, Revelation 20:7–8, Holy Quran Chapter 15: Section 3, Verses 26–40 and Chapter 18: Section 11, Footnotes 1524a–1525a. These Scriptures Identifies God and the Devil! God and the Devil residies within the nature of every human being, and not in the sky or in the ground! *I REPEAT; GOD AND THE DEVIL IS A CONCEPT THAT DESCRIBES THE TWO-SIDED NATURE OF MAN! MASTER-KEY TO THIS BOOK "DIVINE Identity Restored: Isaiah 62:2 and Holy Quran C.95, 2767"*

The next step in the Restoration of Birthright for the Blackman and Woman of America is "Giving the Whiteman back his Names, and Regaining their Original Black Names; Names represent Identity!" *The War of Armageddon is a Spiritual War of Choosing your Identity in God, or Choosing your Identity in the Devil.* If you accept your Identity in God, then he will show you what your Name is by giving you one of his holy attributes; then your duty is to strive throughout your life to live up to that attribute or Name of God! For you, Sister or Brother, The War of Armageddon for your Soul, has finally ended!! Now, it is time for Everlasting Advancement through Divine Revelation! It is a God-given Birthright of every people to have their Own Economy or Money System.

CHAPTER I
Abraham: The Children of Israel (History of Black People in Scripture)

Abraham

According to the King James Version of the Bible, Abram's father "Terah", moved his family from the land of Ur of the Chaldees, to go into the land of Canaan, however, they came into Haran, and dwelt there. The Lord, said unto Abram, get thee out of this country, and from thy father's house unto a land that I will show you. Genesis 12:2–3 And I will make of thee a great nation, and I will bless thee, and make thy name great; and thou shall be a blessing;

3. And I will bless them that bless thee, and curse them that curseth thee: and in thee shall all families of the earth be blessed. Abram departed as God had spoken to him, and he took his nephew Lot, his wife Sarai or Sarah, and all his substance that he had accumulated and left Haran, and went into the land of Canaan. Genesis 15:12–15 And when the sun was going down, a deep sleep fell upon Abram; and, lo, a horror of great darkness fell upon him. And he said unto Abram, "Know of a surety that thy seed shall be a stranger in a land that is not theirs, and shall serve them; and they shall afflict them for four hundred years; "And also that nation, whom they shall serve, will I judge: and afterward shall they come out with great substance.

But Abram's wife Sarai had no children, and she had an Egyptian handmaid named Hagar. Sarai gave Hagar to Abram to be his wife, and she conceived a child and named him Ishmael. And God said unto Abraham, that he should not call his wife Sarai, but her name shall be Sarah. Also that he would bless her with a child and his name would be Isaac. Abraham had a feast the same day that Isaac was weaned from Sarah, and Sarah saw Ishmael mocking the fact that she was too old to be weaning, and asked Abraham to cast out Hagar and Ishmael. Abraham was grieved; but God said, do not grieve because he was going to make a great nation out of Ishmael and Isaac; both were his seeds!

Abraham was a prophet of God, and did many things to prove his love and loyalty to God. One example, Abraham was going to sacrifice his son Isaac on the altar for a burnt offering but God's Angel stopped him saying "now I knowest that thou fearest God", do not lay thine hand upon the lad. Abraham was an upright person, that feared God. He was not given a scripture as such, but his religion was entire submission to the will of God, regardless as to what it was. There is no detailed knowledge of a religion as it is today. Once Abraham submitted to God, he became the recipient of the Covenant with God that he become the "Spiritual" father of all the Nations. His seed would inherit the earth; however, "Know of surety that thy seed shall be a stranger in a land that is not theirs for four hundred years.

His actual seed, Ishmael, was promised by God to make a great nation out of him. Isaac was also to be blessed with a great nation and the history of the evolution of this side of Abraham's seed will cover much of our story. Abraham gave all that he had to Isaac, he live one hundred and fifteen years; and was gathered to his people. And his sons Isaac and Ishmael buried him in the cave of Machpelah. And it came to pass after the death of Abraham, that God blessed his son Isaac.

Isaac

Genesis 26: 2–3 And the Lord appeared unto him, and said, go not down into Egypt; dwell in the land which I shall tell thee of.

3. Sojourn in this land, and I will be with thee, and will bless thee; for unto thee, and unto thy seed, I will give all these countries, and I will perform the oath which I sware unto Abraham thy father. Because that Abraham obeyed my voice, and kept my charge, my commandments, my statures, and my laws.

When Isaac was forty years old, he took a wife, named Rebekah. Isaac asked the Lord to allow his wife to conceive because she was barren. She conceived and the Lord told her that she had two nations (twins) in her womb, and that one people would be stronger than the other people, and the elder shall serve the younger. The elder son's name was Esau and he was hairy all over. The younger son's name was Jacob and he was smooth. Isaac loved Esau and he was a cunning man of the field. Rebekah loved Jacob and he was a man that dwelled in tents. One day Esau came from the field feeling faint and asked his brother Jacob for some food. Jacob said to Esau "Sell me thy birthright" and Esau said what good is a birthright is he die from hunger, so he sold his birthright to Jacob.

Now when Isaac was old, he called his son Esau to him, and said I know not when death will overtake me so go to the field, take some venison prepare it, that I may eat so that I may bless you before I die. Rebekah heard this and told her son Jacob to put on hairy clothes, prepare the venison, and pretend that he was Esau in order to get Esau's blessing. Jacob did as his mother told him and deceived his father Isaac into giving Esau's blessing to him. Esau returned and found out what had happened and hated Jacob even more than ever. First he took his Birthright and now his Blessing. Esau left and went unto

Ishmael; Abraham's other son! (This connection will reappear later on in the story.

Jacob took two wives, Rachel and Leah. Jacob had seven children from Leah, six sons and one daughter. Rachel had two sons; Joseph and Benjamin. four sons from two women servants which makes a total of thirteen children. One night, Jacob was left alone and he wrestle with a man (angel) all night until he could get a blessing, and the man (angel) said, what is your name? My name is Jacob, well, your name shall no more be Jacob, but Israel. Thus, we now have Israel, and later the Children of Israel. Don't forget how this Nation came about through lying to Isaac and taking Esau's birthright. Isaac was one hundred and eighty years old when de died, he was buried by his sons Esau and Jacob (Israel).

Joseph

Now, we begin with the generation of Jacob. Joseph was a lad of seventeen when he dreamed a dream, and he told it to his brothers. His brothers hated him and when they heard the dream, they hated him even more. Joseph said, behold, we were binding sheaves in the field, and lo, my sheaf arose, and also stood upright; and behold, your sheaves stood round about, and made obeisance to my sheaf. Genesis 37: 5–8 And his brothers said to him, shall thy indeed reign over us? Or shall thy indeed have dominion over us? and they hated him yet the more for his dreams, and for his words. And Joseph dream another dream that the Sun, Moon, and the eleven stars made obesiance to him. He told it to his father and his father rebuked him saying; Shall I and your mother, and brothers bow down to you? Now Jacob loved Joseph and had made him a coat of many colors!

It came to pass, Joseph was with his bothers and they stripped Joseph of his coat of many colors and cast him into a pit. They lifted up their eyes, and said look, a company of Ishmaelites (Ishmael) with spices and myrrh going to Egypt. Why kill him? Let us sell him to the Ishmaelites. Joseph was sold to the Ishmaelites for twenty pieces of silver, and they brought Joseph into Egypt. The brothers took Joseph coat and killed a kid (goat) and smeared the blood all over the coat and took it to their father. They told Jacob that Joseph had been killed, and he mourned the loss of his son.

Joseph was brought to Egypt, and Potiphar, an officer of Pharaoh, an Egyptian captain of the guard, bought him from the Ishmaelites. He saw that the Lord was with him so he made him (Joseph) overseer of his house. From that day forth, the master's house prospered because of Joseph. Later, it came to pass, the master's wife found favor in Joseph and asked him to "lie with me", Joseph refused, and she caught his garment as he fled. She showed the torn garment to her husband saying "Joseph tried to lie with me, and I cried out and he fled leaving this piece of garment behind. Joseph was falsely accused, however, his master, Potiphar, cast him into prison.

Joseph was cast into prison with the king's prisoners and the keeper of the prisoners saw that the Lord was with Joseph so he made him the overseer of the prisoners. The butler and the baker of the King of Egypt had offended him and he cast them into prison where Joseph was kept. One night, the butler and baker had a dream and Joseph asked them to tell him the dream whereas the interpretation belongs to God. The butler said; In my dream, A vine was before me, and in the vine were three branches, and it budded, and her blossoms shot forth; and the clusters brought forth ripe grapes; And Pharaoh's cup was in my hand, and I took the grapes and pressed them into Pharaoh's cup, and I gave the cup to Pharaoh. Joseph said, this is the interpretation; The three branches are three days; within three days, Pharaoh shall lift up thine head, and restore thee to thy place, and you shall deliver Pharaoh his cup after the same manner when you were his butler.

Joseph asked that the butler mention his plight to Pharaoh when he is restored to Pharaoh's good graces.

The chief baker saw that the interpretation was good, so he said; I also had a dream, I had three white baskets on my head, and the top basket had all kinds of bake goods for Pharaoh, and the birds came and ate the bread from the basket that was on my head. Joseph said, this is the interpretation of the dream. The three baskets are three days, and within three days, Pharaoh shall lift up your head and hang you from a tree, and the birds shall eat the flesh from off thee. And the third day, it came to pass because it was Pharaoh's birthday and he made a feast unto all his servants; He lifted up the head of his chief butler and baker. The butler, he restored to his butlership again, and the butler gave Pharaoh his cup. However he hanged the baker, just as Joseph predicted. The butler did not mention Joseph to Pharaoh, but rather forgot him. After two years, Pharaoh had a dream that no one in his Kingdom could interpret; including his wise men and magicians. It was then that the butler remembered Joseph, and he explained to pharaoh that while in prison a young man interpreted his and the baker's dreams; He was still in prison and Pharaoh sent for Joseph!

Pharaoh said to Joseph, I have had a dream and I understand that you can interpret it. Joseph said to Pharaoh that it is not in me but up to God. Phararaoh said, I stood by the bank of the river and out of the river came seven fat, well favored kines (cows) and fed in the meadow. And, then, seven ill favored, lean kines did come up and ate the first fat kine. And, when they had eaten them up, it could not be noticed that they had eaten the other kine. So I awoke. And I saw seven ears came up on one stark, full and good. And, behold, seven ears, blasted, withered, and thin with the east wind sprung u after them. The thin ears devoured the seven good ears. I told this to the wise men and magicians and no one can interpret it.

Joseph said that your dream is one dream; God has showed Pharaoh what he about to do. The seven good ears and the seven fat kine are seven years. The seven thin kine and the seven empty ears seven years of famine. What God is about to do, he has showed to Pharaoh so he can prepare himself. First, there will be seven yeras of plenty throughout the land of Egypt, and then there will be seven years of famine that will be very greivous. Pharaoh must seek out a man discreet and wise in the land to collect a fifth of all that is produced during the plentiful years and store it against the years of famine that is sure to come. Each city should gather this food, appoint officers as overseers so that Egypt will not perish during the famine. Pharaoh said that inasmuch as God has shown you my dream (the interpretation), then there is none more discreet or wise as you, therefore, you shall be over my household, and according to your word shall all my people be ruled, and only I shall be greater than you. Pharaoh made Joseph ruler over all of Egypt. He gave Joseph a wife named Asenath. He was arrayed in fine lined, a gold chain, and Pharaoh took off his ring and put it on Joseph's hand. Joseph gathered food for seven years, and laid it up in the cities. And unto Joseph was born two sons before the years of the famine came. The first-born was named Manasseh; meaning God made me forget all my toil, and all my father's house. The second son was named Ephraim; meaning God has caused me to be fruitful in the land of my afflictions.

After the seven years of plenty in the land, then came the famine, but in Egypt, there was bread. The famine was all over the earth, so all countries came to Pharaoh, and Pharaoh sent them to Joseph. Israel sent ten of his sons to buy corn in Egypt, and kept behind Benjamin so that nothing would happen to him. However, Joseph accused them of spying and said that he would keep one brother as hostage until they proved their innocence by bringing the other members of the family to him. Israel (Jacob) was persuaded to send Benjamin the second time; (which makes eleven brothers) and they bowed down to Joseph, thus fulfilling his dream. Joseph made himself known to his brothers and they rejoiced. He sent for his father and Joseph explained that there was no need for anyone to grieve because God had sent him forward to preserve life by a great deliverance. It was not the brothers that sent him to Egypt, but rather God, and he had made him Lord over Pharaoh house, and ruler throughout the land.

While in Egypt, Israel predicted what would happen to his sons, and their offsprings. Israel died and was buried in the land of Canaan with his forefathers. Joseph lived to be one hundred and ten years old and he was embalmed and put in a coffin in Egypt. And now, begins the interesting story of the development and evolution of the Children of Israel. The Children of Israel will fulfill the stolen birthright (Act as though they are the rightful heirs to the Kingdom of God), and receive all the blessings (Riches), that their father (Jacob) tricked away from his brother Esau. But remember, Isaac told Esau, Genesis 27:40 And by thy sword shall thy live, and shall serve thy brother: and it shall come to pass when thy shall have the dominion, that thy shall break his yoke from off thy neck. This dominion of Jacob (Children of Israel) shall last for 6,000 years. From the time of Abraham, Isaac, Jacob, and now the Children of Israel up to today there was a history that should be understood as to how the Children of Israel acquired their destiny; through tricks and lies, and therfore that is how they will rule the nations of the earth. It is this type of rulership that will cause God to send other Prophet into the world to bring about the spiritual "Resurrection Of The Dead."

CHAPTER II
Historical View—The Truth About Moses—Children of Israel (The Ten Commandments)

Adam and Eve and This Children of Israel are White People

Genesis 1:26–28 And God said "Let us make man in our own image after our likeness, let them have dominion over the fowl of the air and over all the earth." And God said unto them, "Be fruitful and multiply and replenish the earth and subdue it." According to the Bible, Adam and Eve (Children of Israel) were expelled from the Garden of Eden (Egypt) for disobeying God and was banished into the earth (Wilderness) to till the ground from where he was taken. After man (Children of Israel was driven out of the Garden of Eden, God placed at the east of the Garden of Eden a cherubin, with a flaming sword which turned every way to protect the way of life of the Black People of Eden from the tricks and lies (tricknology) of White People.

The Children of Israel were driven into the wilderness (Hills and Caves of West Asia) and because of their disobedience they were deprived of a religious guide or leader from God. Moses did not come to this people until 2,000 years later! This was in order to fulfill the promise that God made Abraham, Isaac, and Jacob that these people would rule the earth; for a time. Also this was the new people that God would make through Moses. As of now, they are being punished for disobeying God in the Garden and this life in the wilderness will condition them to listen to the next guide that God will send them; Which will be Moses.

During the time that the Children of Israel were in Egypt, they had become a part of the total fabric of government and society. They were not all toiling the soil and slaves. Many were merchants and businessmen, clerks and politicians. They also were thieves, liars, and murderers! When the level of chaos became unbearable; God put it in the heart of the King to exile them so that they could start their own government and thus fulfill prophecy. Now, remember, they had rejected God and his ways (Garden of Eden) and now they were starting on their own; i.e. according to their own knowledge of how life (Government) operates. From Abraham to Moses is a 2,000 year period. Now, we begin with the Children of Israel (Adam and Eve; A New Nation) in the caves and hillsides of Europe. Bible calls it the wilderness!

Children of Israel in Exile (White People)

Children of Israel was exiled into the hills and caves of West Asia (They now call it Europe). They were without anything to start civilization and became savages. They remained in such condition for two thousand years—no guide or literature. They lost all knowledge of civilization. Man did not start or was created by God from the Monkey, but rather all the monkey family were from this two thousand year period as a result of co-habitation with the beasts and living a savage life.

Being deprived of Diving Guidance for their disobedience; the making of mischief, and causing confusion in the Garden of Eden, this developed within the Children of Israel A Savage State of Mind! They became so savage that they lost all their sense of shame. They started going nude as they are doing today. They became shameless. In the winter they wore animal skins for clothes, and grew hair all over their bodies and faces like all the other wild animals. In those days, they made their homes in the caves on hill-sides. They had it very hard trying to save themselves from being destroyed by wild beasts that were plentiful at that time in Europe.

Being without a guide, they started walking on their hands and feet like all animals; and, learned to climb trees as good as any of the animals. At night, they would climb up into trees, carrying large stones and clubs to keep the animals from eating their families. Their next and best weapons were the dogs. They tamed some of these dogs to live in the caves with families to help protect them from the wild beasts. After a time, the dog held a high place among the family because of his fearlessness to attack the enemies of his master. Today, the dog is still loved, and is called man's best friend This comes from the cave days.

Moses

After two thousand years of living like a savage, God raised up Moses to bring these people (Israelites) into civilization to take their place as rulers of the "New Way Of Life for Man; Unrighteousness", as God had intended for them. REMEMBER, GOD ALLOWED THESE THINGS TO HAPPEN SO THAT MAN CAN LEARN FROM THE ERRORS OF HIS WAYS THROUGH EXPERIENCE—AN NOT JUST BELIEF! Divine Consciousness is Within; Not in the Sky. Moses became their God and Leader. He brought them out of the caves; taught them to believe in God; taught them to wear clothes; how to cook food; how to season it with salt; what beef they should kill and eat; and how to use fire for their service. Moses taught them against putting the female cow under burden. He established for them, Friday as the day to eat fish, and not to eat meat (beef) on that day. And, fish is the main menu in many of the homes today on Fridays. They were so evil (savage) that Moses had to build a ring of fire around him at night; and he would sleep in the middle of the ring (center) to keep them from harming him. They were afraid of fire and are still afraid of fire.

One day, Moses told them that he was going to have fish come up from the sea that night so that tomorrow they will have some fish. One the next day, the fish were there. Moses had a boatload sent up from Egypt. Moses said, "See, the sea came up last night and brought us some fish!" One of the savages was a little smart and he said to Moses, "Where is the water?" From then on, Moses recognized the fact that he could not say just anything to them. He had a very hard time trying to civilize them. Once, they gave Moses so much trouble that he took a few sticks of dynamite, went up on the mountainside, placed them into the ground and went back to get the ones giving the most trouble. He said to them, "Stand there on the edge of this mountain and you will hear the voice of God." They stood there about 300 in number, Moses set the fuse off and it killed all of them.

Moses taught the Children of Israel (Savages) that if they would follow and obey him that they would rule world. Most of them believed Moses just to get out of the caves. They were given the knowledge and power to bring every living thing, regardless of its kind of life, into subjection. And God said, "Let us make man in our image after our likeness, let them have dominion over the fish of the sea and over the fowl of the air and over the cattle and over all the earth and subdue it." (Genesis 1:26, 28) The above all was necessary if they were to rule as a God of the world. They must conquer, and bring into subjection all life upon the earth—not land life alone, but they must subdue the sea, master everything, until a greater master or God comes, which would mean the end of their power over the live of the earth. This is the new man that god had Moses to make! Children of Israel.

In the past 4,000 years up to today, these people have subdued every kind of living thing upon the earth. God has blessed them to exercise all their knowledge and blessed them with guides (Prophets) and with the rain and seasons of the earth. Today their wealth is great upon the earth. Their sciences of worldly goods have sent them, not only after the wealth of other than their own people, but even after the lives and property of their own kind. They have tried to re-people (replenish) the earth with their own kind by mixing their blood into every race. But the job is too big for them to ever conquer. The guidance that Moses left this race of people was five books: Genesis (Beginning of their Civilization), Exodus (Laws on how to leave uncleanliness and how to be civilized), Leviticus (Laws and ceremonies of Government), Numbers (Census of the people) and Deuteronomy (Prophecies about their doom and end of their civilization).

Before Jesus came to these people 2,000 years later, it was already written in the history who they were. What their intentions were in the Bible: St. John 8:38–44 wherein Jesus said, "I speak that which I Have seen with my father. Ye do the deeds of your father and ye do that which you have seen with your father. They said to him, we are not born of fornication, we have one father, even God. Jesus said unto them, "If God were your father, ye would love me; ye are of your father the devil, and the lust of your father ye will do." He was a murderer from the beginning and abide not in the truth because there is no truth in him. But now, let us go to the life of Jesus and continue our story of The Israelites, and the evolution of Divine REVELATION.

In the Book of Exodus, (meaning to exit from unclean living), Moses left them with many laws to live by but the most famous is:

The Ten Commandments

1. Thou shall have no other Gods before me, i.e.(Idolatry forbidden) also, Thou shall not make unto thee any graven images; (Pictures or Statues).

2. Thou shall not bow down thyself to them, nor serve them.
3. Thou shall not take the name of the Lord thy God in vain.
4. Remember the Sabbath day, to keep it holy
5. Honor thy father and thy mother; that thy days may be long upon the land which the Lord thy God giveth thee.
6. Thou shall not kill.
7. Thou shall not commit adultery.
8. Thou shall not steal.
9. Thou shall not bear false witness against thy neighbor.
10. Thou shall not covet thy neighbor's house, wife, manservant, ox, nor his ass, nor anything that is thy neighbor's.

The five books of Moses, including the Ten Commandments, were Moses' contribution to Mankind in God's revelation on how Man should live. The Laws, Covenant, and Judgements against the Israelites were sealed in a book. Genesis 31:26–29 Take this book of the law, and put it in the side of the Ark of the Covenant, that it may be there as a witness against thee. For I know that after my death, ye will utterly corrupt yourselves, and turn aside from the way which I have commanded you. The names of the Children of Israel are Joseph (Sons; Ephraim and Manasseh), Benjamin, Reuben, Simeon, Levi, Juda, Issachar, Zebulun, Dan, Naphtali, Gad, and Asher.

CHAPTER III
The "Life" of Jesus Christ (Life Stages: Mary and Joseph, Spiritually, Ministry, Crucifiction, and Resurrection)

Physical Birth of Jesus Christ (Mary and Joseph)

Moses' civilization did not last 2,000 years but rather 1,700 years and Nimrod, the Wicked, who captured the City of Ninevah, and ruled it for three hundred years. He ruled the last of the two thousand years. Then the people grew more and more away from the law, as Moses had given it to them and they didn't want to keep it, and did not keep it. This Nimrod kept up trouble for the people. He made wars and revolution for them for many years. Nimrod was born December 25, and this is the man that the Christians worship every 25th day of December and say that it is Jesus. Jesus was not born on this date, not even in the month of December.

After Moses' 2,000 years, then came Jesus. His mother name was Mary and his father's name was Joseph. Mary and Joseph were school children together. They always loved each other. They agreed to marry when very small children going to school. When Joseph and Mary grew to the age of 15 and 17, Joseph went to Mary's father and told him that he loved Mary and Mary loved him, that they wanted to marry. Joseph was a poor man, a common liver. He also was a carpenter by trade, not a first class carpenter, but one of those rough building little rough houses in South Europe.

Mary's father was rich and had plenty. Also, her grandfather was rich. So, Mary's father objected to her marriage to Joseph, a poor carpenter. Mary loved Joseph and told her father that she did not care if Joseph didn't have anything. She loved him and if she did not marry him, she would not marry anyone else. When the old man heard this it made him sick because no father wants his daughter to be a old maid. Joseph gave up thinking about marrying Mary and went and married another girl. Mary's father would go out and bring in very rich young men for his daughter in hopes of his daughter taking a-liking to some of these young men, but she did not.

Joseph owned a little house, a small piece of land and also going rearing up a little family. He soon was the father of six children by this girl that he married, and was married to her six years. As Mary's father was a big wealthy man, also a great architect, one who designs or draws plans for buildings. The old man had to go away to another town, about 25 miles from his home and set up a Temple, but before he left home, he called Mary and said to her, "Now daughter, I have to go away and I will be gone for about three days." "Now you must take care of everything until I return." You must feed and water all of the livestock (for the old man had plenty of cattle). He also said to Mary, "I want you to wear my old clothes and put on some false whiskers and the people when they see you going down to feed the stock, they will think you are me and no-one will say anything to you..."

After the old man leaves on his journey, a great dust storm came up which made it very dark. This kind of storm comes up twice a year. During this storm, Mary becomes frightened and sends a message to Joseph telling him that her father had gone away and that he would be away for three days, and that she was left to feed and water all of the livestock and that she was alone and was a little afraid and she asked Joseph to come over and help her to take care of everything and that he would be company for her. Joseph tells his wife that he has to go off on a little business. He came over to Mary's house and she tells him of the costumes of her fathers that she should wear when she goes out to feed the stocks.

Joseph said, "Give me the old man's costume and when anybody sees us, they will think I am the old man with you." Joseph gets the team ready and Mary gets in with him. Off they went to feed the stock. The next day Joseph came back and stayed with Mary and helped her to feed and take care of the stock again. And the third day, the old man came back and asked his daughter, how was everything? She said alright father. So after three months the old man noticed Mary was growing larger than usual. He said to Mary, "What is the matter with you fattening so fast, are you eating more than you should?" Mary said, "No, Father, I am not eating more than I should. The old man called Mary again and said, "Mary, there is something the matter with you." Look how large you are. What are you doing? Mary no longer could hide it, so she told him the truth.

She said to him, "Father, do you remember when you went off to set up a Temple and stayed three days some time ago and left me to attend the livestock?" Well, I was afraid because of such a duststorm and sent for Joseph to come over and help me. Well, he came and did help me feed the stock. The old man said, "Yes, and he fed them too." She said to him, Do you remember Joseph and me were trying to get you to let us marry when we were young and you would not?" Now this is what happened and I shall send for Joseph and let him tell you for himself. An old woman had already been to Joseph and told him that the child Mary was with was his child and that the child would be a wonderful child, a Prophet and Teacher, and this child is your child but Joseph denied it.

But this woman knew because she was a Prophetist, or what we call a medium. She told him his name was in the Holy Quran and that he should take care of him and that the authorities would seek the child's life. Joseph goes and tell Mary the good news what the old woman had told him concerning the child. Then Joseph went to Mary's father. By this time the old man was real sick because Mary was growing larger and larger every-day and he was in bed and he had just about pulled all of the whiskers out of his chin. Joseph said to the old man, "I will tell you about the whole thing, then you can kill me, right here. Mary and I always loved each other, even when we were going to school and promised to marry when we were old enough and I came to you and asked you for Mary and you would not give her to me. Now this is what happened. I am the father of the child that Mary is with, but remember that the child is going to be a great man, A Prophet and Teacher. His name can be found in the history of the Holy Quran. Now remember, you must not tell anyone about this because of the authorities. If they knew this they would kill the child so keep your mouth shut about this, and now you can kill me if you want to. I have told the truth.

The nine months of Mary's pregnancy drew near the end but the authorities did not know what time the child would be born. So the same medium that told Joseph of the child, also goes and tell the authorities but no-one knew which day the child would be born, but they knew the week. The authorities had a Committee to go around and take Census of all the pregnant women and what time they should birth. This committee took a check-up of everyone that was pregnant with a child. When the week came that Jesus should be born, the authorities had given orders that all boy babies born in that week should be killed. Joseph came and took charge of Mary himself. All men over in Asia are taught how to take care of their wives and perform this duty for their wives. In case they don't care for a wet nurse, the girls are also taught when very young.

Mary's father had stock of all kind and down off from the house, he had stalls built, one joining each other and hay racks. Joseph took one of the stalls and filled it in all around the inside and put a bed in the center for Mary (This is the Manger that the Bible speaks about where Jesus was born). To look at the stalls from the outside, it looked as if it was just a stall filled with hay for the stock. In this way he concealed Mary from the authorities. He brought her food and water everyday. In that week when the authorities was expecting Jesus to be born, they sent the committee around to those who had a list of that would give birth to child in the same week. When they came to Mary's father's house, they knocked on the door and the old man goes and meet them. The said to him, "Where is the woman that got a baby this week?" "Doesn't she stay here?" The old man said "What woman?" They said, "The one that was with child." He said, "Oh, I know what you are talking about." The woman that was here some time ago." she was only visiting here, the old man said. "She has returned to her home in Egypt." They said, "Oh, she was just visiting?" The old man said, "Yes that is all." So the committee marked Mary off of their list as one that was only visiting.

Joseph came daily with water and food to Mary and to see the baby. He fooled his wife by telling her that he had a job building a house. THIS IS HOW JESUS WAS BORN!

Birth of Jesus (Spiritually)

Jesus was born a normal birth by two ordinary human beings (his mission is Divine; but his birth was human). His mother's name was Mary and his father's name was Joseph. Jesus was conceived and born out of wedlock, and he was raised by his mother Mary. His father Joseph was already married to another woman and had six children. Jesus was born out of wedlock as a sign of something to come. (A great nation would be born out of wedlock from another people and it would take God and his spirit to raise them up to their natural state in life). The same thing happened to Jesus, he was born an outcast so that God could prove that—he was his Son spiritually and fulfilling the prophecy that he was the last prophet to the Jews. Just as the So-Called Negroes are outcast in America, they will be the last people that God will chose to carry his message to the world. BELIEVE IT OR NOT!

Mary and Joseph were school children together, and were in love, they promised to marry when they came of age at 17 and 15. Joseph was a poor carpenter, while Mary's father was a rich architect. When Joseph came to him and asked for Mary's hand, he refused. Mary was heartbroken and said that she would never marry anyone, if not Joseph. In the meantime, Joseph gave up thinking about Mary and went and married another girl. Joseph owned a little piece of land, a home, and soon he was the father of six children by this girl, and was married six years. When Jesus had accepted his mission from God, he had this to say about his mother and brothers. Matthews 12:46, 47, 50 "While he yet talked to the people, behold, his mother and his brethren stood /outside/, desiring to speak with him, 47 Then one said unto him, Behold, thy mother and thy brethen stand /outside/ desiring to speak with thee. 48. But he answered and said unto him that told him, who is my mother? And who are my brethren? 49 And he stretched forth his hands toward his disciples, and said Behold my mother and my brethren! 50 For whosoever shall do the will of my Father, who is in heaven, the same is my brother, and sister, and mother. "He still did not deny that was his mother and brethren standing outside!"

In the East, a great dust storm comes up twice a year; Mary's father was away on business and she sent for Joseph to keep her company because she was frightened. Joseph came and stayed three days. After three months, Mary's father noticed that she was getting fat and he confronted her. Mary confessed and sent for Joseph to explain everything. An old woman had already been to Joseph and explained to him that the child was his child, and would grow up to be a great man. A Teacher and a Prophet. His name was written in the Holy Quran. He should take care of the child because the authorities would try to kill him because they think he is going to change the government. The Bible explains it like this Matthews 1:20–21

20. But while he thought on these, behold /an angel/ of the Lord appeared unto him in a dream, saying Joseph, thou son of David, fear not to take unto thee Mary, thy wife; for that which is conceived in her is of the Holy /Spirit/.

21. And she shall bring forth a son, and thou shall call his name Jesus; for he shall save his people from their sins.

Joseph hurried to her father and explained every thing; That if he had allowed him to marry Mary, this would not have happened, but, the child is going to be a great man and they must protect Mary and the child from the authorities. The nine months drew near, but the authorities did not know the time exactly, but they knew the week. A Census Committee was sent around to check all pregnant women. Mary was kept hiding in a stall built off from the house, joining one another and some hay stacks. Joseph took one of the stalls and fill it in all around the inside, and put a bed in the center for Mary. This was the way he concealed Mary from the authorities. When the authorities inquired of Mary, her father said "Oh" that woman was just visiting from Cairo. (This is the Manger that's mentioned in the Bible that Jesus was born in).

The actual day that Jesus was born, no one knows because it was kept a secret for his protection. We do know it was in Autumn! The Holy Quran describes the time and child-birth like this. Holy Quran Ch.19 V. 1539–1939a "Mary gave birth to Jesus under the ordinary circumstances which women experience in giving birth to children. The throes of childbirth were too sever for her to bear, and hence she uttered such words: Oh, would that I had died before this, and had been a thing quite forgotten. The reference to the throes of childbirh clearly shows that an ordinary child was coming into the world. The Quran does not accept that Jesus was born on 25th of December. It was the time when fresh ripe dates are found on palm trees. Read Chapter 19, titled Mary and Jesus; Holy Quran.

After the baby was born Mary took her child and went to Cairo, Egypt to live with some of her people; while Jesus went to school. At the age of 12, Jesus met an old man coming from school, who taught him about his mission in life. He told Jesus that his name was in the Holy Quran, and that after he finish school he would go to Europe and finish teaching the Jews the laws that Moses began teaching them 2000 years ago. However, you must know how to take care of yourself because they will try to kill you. They think that you will tear down what Moses built for them. The old man taught Jesus the Radio In The Head or "Telepathy; the ability to send and receive messages, in the head. At the age of 14, his mother, could not keep him any longer. The day he left for Europe, she gave him two thousand dollars, and he had not gone but a few blocks before he had given it all away.

He never ate a meal without working for it, but once, and that was one day he walked until his feet was so sore and swollen that he couldn't work. He stopped at this woman's house, by the name of Martha, (Luke 10:38) She bath his feet, and prepared him some food. This is not the only time that he was in her home. Now Martha had a sister named Mary, and a brother named Lazarus, and it is important to understand the story of Lazarus and the Resurrection, because most of the world has misunderstood Jesus and his Ministry.

Remember, Jesus was not born on Christmas, December 25, but rather the first or second week in September.

Birth of Jesus and his Ministry: Resurrection of The Dead!

The Jewish view that Jesus was conceived in sin and illegitimate and the Christian view that he was God or the Son of God who had entered Mary's womb, are two views not accepted by the Holy Quran. For example, Luke 1:26:31–34 King James Version of the Bible.

26. And in the sixth month the angel, Gabriel, was sent from God unto a city of Galilee, named Nazareth.

27. To a virgin espoused (to be married) to a man whose name was Joseph, of the House of David; and the virgin's name was Mary.

28. And the angel came in unto her, and said, Hail, thou who art highly favored, the Lord is with thee; blessed art thou among women.

29. And when she saw him, she was troubled at his saying, and considered in her mind, what manner of greeting this should be.

30. And the angel said unto her, Fear not, Mary; for thou hast found favor with God.

31. And behold, thou shall conceive in thou womb, and bring forth a son, and shall call his name JESUS.

34. Then said Mary unto the angel, How shall this be, seeing I know not a man?

Holy Quran 3:46 verse She said: My Lord, how can I have a son and man has not touched me? He said: even so; Allah creates what he pleases. Where he decrees a matter, He only says to it, Be and it is. Now the explanation! 427 Mary's espousal had yet to be decided, and perhaps she had not been informed of this when she was given the good news of a son being born to her. Hence she says that man had not touched her yet. And she was told in reply, "Even so"; i.e., the child will be born by God bringing about the circumstances which result in the birth of a child. The words do not show that she would conceive out of the ordinary course of nature. No words from the angel or Mary proves anything except the fact that Mary was to give birth to a son in accordance with the prophecy. The whole of creation is brought about by the Divine Word of Allah (God) but it is always in accord with the Laws of Nature. (Jesus was no exception)! Jesus was raised as any other normal child, went to school, and was informed of his mission in life (already in the book). Before beginning the Ministry of Jesus, always remember that the chief characteristic of Jesus speeches is that he spoke in parables, and clothed his ideas in allegorical language.

Holy Quran, Chapter 22, Verse 1671, The Judgement; In the Holy Quran, the word "Raising" is used in three senses (1) the raising of the dead to life according to their good or evil deed on the Judgement Day; (2) the raising of the spiritually dead to life by the prophets; and (3) the raising up of prophets by Allah for the guidance of mankind. In the case of Jesus and Lazarus; then number two and three applies. Jesus was a Prophet raised by God (Allah) for the purpose of guiding Mankind; and now the story of Lazarus and the Resurrection. The various stages that every human being pass through in his evolution to perfection is referred to as a Resurrection. Just as the physical evolution of a man is gradual, so is his spiritual growth and development.

St. John 11:1–44 Now a certain man was sick named Lazarus, of Bethany, the town of Mary and her sister Martha. 3 Therefore his sisters sent unto him (Jesus), saying Lord, behold, he whom thou lovest is sick. 4 When Jesus heard that, he said, this sickness is not unto death, but for the glory of God, that the Son of God might be glorified by it. 11 These things said he and after that he said unto them, our friend Lazarus sleepeth; but I go that I may awake him out of his sleep. Notice that Jesus (A Prophet) said that Lazarus was asleep (Spiritually Asleep to God and he would wake him up) Then said Jesus unto them plainly, Lazarus is dead. (Spiritually dead, and not Physically dead).

15 And I am glad for your sake that I was not there, to the intent that you may believe; nevertherless, let us go unto him. 21 Then Martha said unto Jesus, Lord if thou hadst been here, my brother had not died. 22 But I know that even now, whatever thou will ask of God, God will give it to thee. 25 Jesus said unto her, I am the Resurrection (The raising of the spiritually dead to life by the prophets) and the life; he that believeth in me, though he was dead, yet shall he live. 26 And whosover liveth and believeth in me, shall never die. Believest thou this? What Jesus meant was this. If a person is spiritually alive to the knowledge of the true and living god and his representative (Jesus) and believeth in him, then he would never die (spiritually), and if he is dead to the knowledge of God and Jesus, but start to Believe in him, then even he could come alive and live (Mentally and Spiritually in God) through the knowledge of his servant, Jesus.

40 Jesus said unto her, said I not unto thee, that if thou wouldest believe, thou shouldest see the glory of God? And when he thus had spoken he cried with a loud voice. Lazarus come forth. 44 And he that was dead (spiritually) came forth, bound hand and foot with graveclothes; and his face was bound with a cloth. Jesus said unto them, loose him and let him go. This is a story of a man, Lazarus, sleeping in his "mental grave of ignorance" about himself, and was living the life of a dead man (no progress or achievement). His sisters knew that Jesus could raise him back to spiritual and mental life, because they had seen his works, but Lazarus was dead to the Truth of who Jesus really was! But in the end when Jesus called with a loud voice, Lazarus recognized the voice and believed, and came forth to life. Lazarus was sick spiritually, and it took Jesus to raise him spiritually. Lazarus was never "PHYSICALLY DEAD! He was "DEAD SPIRITUALLY"!

Jesus said that, he that believeth in me though he was spiritually dead before I arrived on the scene, yet shall he live. Belief is the magic that causes the spiritually dead to rise or the "dead to come forth out of their graves; mental graves. Belief is what make the "Blind to See" and the "Lame to Walk". Belief in God enables the spiritually blind to see and the mentally lame or mental cripple, to walk upright with Truth. These miracles came about because of the Belief in God, and is a testimony that the Divinity of God resides within Man. This is where the term; Son Of God comes from, Man is like a "Son" to the Almighty and he protects him if he seeks God's help. If you cannot "see" God in a human being, then it is obvious that you have not been born of God (Spiritually Born). John 1:12–13 But as many received him, to them gave he power to become the Children of God, even to them that believe on his name; 13 Who were born not of Blood, nor of the will of the flesh, nor of the will of man, but of God. If you have been born of God (spiritually), then you have been raised from the dead! This has nothing to do with your physical birth from your parents, but rather your spiritual birth from your Heavenly Father brought about because of your BELIEF in Him and his Prophets.

Crucifiction and Resurrection of Jesus!

After Lazarus, Jesus had many other experiences that were trying to the authorities. Jesus had a hard time trying to teach the people (Jews). He never had over thirty-five people at one time to listen to him (The multitudes in the Bible, only heard of Jesus' teachings). Jesus taught twenty-two years on the run, until finally, he read and understood that he was two-thousand years too soon to bring about a reform. That another one would come, like him, and he would be successful to convert the world to righteousness, (after the wicked has been removed); This man is known as the Second Coming of Jesus; different man but the same mission)

Jesus decided to end his mission. He was teaching outside a Jew's store, and wouldn't leave and the Jew sent for the authorities. There was a twenty-five hundred dollars reward for Jesus if he was dead, and fifteen-hundred dollars if he was alive. The soldiers both grabbed Jesus at the same time and were arguing over who's prisoner he was. Jesus settled the dispute, and said the one on the right touched him one tenth of a second before the other. The soldier told Jesus that he was going to be cut into little pieces, why not let him kill him for the larger reward, Jesus agreed; He stretched out his arms up against a old boarded store. Jesus was very brave; He was stabbed once and turned over to Pilate to be Crucified on the cross! The Bible puts it this way. John 19:34 But one of the soldiers, with a spear, pierced his side, and immediatedly came there out blood and water. AND NOW, THE "SPIRITUAL MEANING" OF THE CRUCIFICTION OF JESUS, as given in the Holy Quran Chapter 4–157.

And for their saying: we have killed the Messiah, Jesus, son of Mary, the messenger of Allah, and they killed him not, nor did they cause his death on the cross, but he was made to appear to them as such, And certainly those who differ therein are in doubt about it. They have no knowledge about it, but only follow a conjecture, and they killed him not for certain. That Jesus died a natural death and not on the cross is plainly stated 5:117 Holy Quran "And I was a witness of them so long as I was among them, but when thou didst cause me to die, Thou were the watcher over them". The Gospel contains clear testimony showing that Jesus Christ escaped death on the cross. The following points may be noted: (1) Jesus remained on the cross for a few hours only (Mark 15:25; John 19:14) But death by crucifiction was always tardy.

(2) The two men crucified with Jesus were still alive when taken down from the cross; the presumption is that Jesus too was alive.

(3) The breaking of legs was resorted to in the case of the two criminals but dispensed with in the case of Jesus (John 19:32,33).

(4) the side of Jesus being pierced, blood rushed out and this was a certain sign of life.

(5) Even Pilate did not believe that Jesus actually died in so short a time (Mark 15:44).

(6) Jesus was not buried like the two criminals, but was given into the charge of a wealthy disciple of his, who lavished care on him and put him in a spacious tomb hewn in the side of a rock (Mark 15:46).

(7) When the tomb was seen on the third day, the stone was found to have been removed from its mouth (Mark 16:4), which would not have been the case if there had been a supernatural rising.

(8) Mary, when she saw him, took him for the gardener.

(9) Such disguise would not have been needed if Jesus had risen from the dead.

(10) It was in the same body of flesh that the disciples saw Jesus, and the wounds were still there deep enough for a man to thrust his hand in (John 20:25-28)

(11) He still felt hunger and ate as his disciples ate (Luke 24:39-43).

(12) Jesus Christ undertook a journey to Galilee with two of his disciples walking side by side with him (Matt 28:10), which shows that he was fleeing for refuge; a journey to Galilee was not necessary to rise to heaven.

(13) In all post crucifiction appearances Jesus is found hiding himself as if he feared being discovered.

(14) Jesus Christ prayed the whole night before his arrest to be saved from the accursed death on the cross, and he also asked his disciples to pray for him; the prayers of a righteous man in distress and affliction are always accepted. He seem to have even received a promise from God to be saved, and it was to this promise that he referred when he cried out on the cross: My God, My God, why hast Thou forsaken me? Heb. 5:7 makes the matter still more clear, for there it is plainly stated that the prayer of Jesus was accepted: "When he had offered up prayers and

supplications with strong crying and tears unto Him who was able to save him from death, and was heard in that he feared."

Jesus did not die on the cross, nor was he killed as were the two thieves, but to the Jews he appeared as if he were dead. Jesus escaped, and died a natural death. After his supposed Death and Resurrection, all types of stories, lies, inuendoes were told on Jesus. The purpose of keeping a supernatural-idea in effect that Jesus came into the world (Not by a Man), and "Died for some Sinners" and he is going to come back again 2,000 years later, at the end of this world, and get the good one and punish the bad ones is designed to keep the masses ignorant. Ask the Jews do they believe this? Ask any intelligent Christian to compare the Holy Quran to any scripture and see the difference. No human being has ever died physically and returned back on the Earth (Including Jesus) to tell us anything! God is Law, and he does not break his laws for Abraham, Moses, Jesus or Muhammad. Jesus said that he came to fulfill Moses Laws, why didn't God let Moses come back to complete his own works? instead of sending Jesus? No, God always sends another person like unto the last prophet to complete a work. Jesus said this about the one coming after him, John 15:25–26 But this cometh to pass, that the word might be fulfilled that is written in their law, they hated me without a cause.

26. But when the comforter is come, whom I will send unto you from the Father, even the Spirit of truth, who proceedeth from the Father, he shall testify of me. And now let us proceed to the one that Jesus referred to as the Comforter, or commonly known in the world as the Second Coming of Jesus. One of his primary objectives is to remove the "veil of ignorance" from the Minds of the Righteous so that they may See and Believe!

One final comment on Jesus and the Resurrection; the teachings that came after Jesus's death are known as "Pie In The Sky" type teachings, and they are not inspired by God (You figure out who inspired this teachings). It goes like this; You (Poor Slave) don't worry about money, homes, or clothes right now, because you will get yours later, after you die, and are resurrected with your Lord and Saviour Jesus Christ. In the meantime, you and your family are hungry, naked, and out of doors. Who is telling you to wait on your reward? There is only one reward, and that is Life, once you are dead, You are done! Why should you believe in another man, when in reality, he is not living the way he tells you. Some of the richest people in America or any where else are Preachers of the Gospel. If a Man won't teach you right in the present; then why should you Believe him about the future. LET THE BUYER BEWARE!

Remember, Jesus spoke of things in an allegorical sense; meaning that he gave a pictorial representation of something that had a deeper spiritual meaning. For instance, Luke 18: 15–17 And they brought unto him also infants, that he would touch them; but when his disciples saw it, they rebuked them. 16 But Jesus called them unto him, and said permit little children to come unto me, and forbid them not; for such is the Kingdom of God. 17 Verily I say unto you, Whosoever shall not receive the Kingdom of God like a little child shall in no way enter it. The deeper meaning that Jesus used these children to demonstrate was that unless an individual becomes as humble and pure in his Heart as a child, he could not enter the deeper Spiritual Kingdom recesses of his Mind. The Kingdom of God is within the Mind of Man.

A final clarification should be made concerning the Jesus of 2,000 years ago. As I said, he did not die "on the cross" but when taken down from cross "HE APPEARED TO BE DEAD", and he was not Crucified, but the "Truth that he brought to the people was Crucified and destroyed". In spiritual terms, if you destroy or crucify what a person stands for, then you have crucified that man. This is what happened to Jesus of 2,000 years ago.

The first Jesus was sent to the Jews, and now the second Jesus will be sent to another people. The Bible explains it like this Revelation 20:3 And cast him into the bottomless pit, and shut him up, and set a seal upon him, that he should deceive the nations no more, till the thousand years should be fulfilled; and after that he must be loosed a little season. After the 1,000 years was up, about 1000 A.D., Mankind was loosed from the confinements of Europe and he began to explore other areas of the world. Some famous explorers like Marco Polo helped established a network of trade-routes between Europe and China. Christopher Columbus discovered a new land called America (All of these discoveries were due to the fact that the Europeans did not know this planet Earth; Who was on it or where they were, so the discovery was on their part; the people living on the land knew who they were all the time). The European trade export was Christianity!

After America was discovered (Another land full of people), England decided that they would need some slaves to do the backbreaking work of developing this new country. The word "slave" was originally applied to "Europeans". It comes from "Slav" a Russian people captured by the Germans. However, Europeans, bought a trading post in the jungles of Africa to lure, buy, kidnap and steal people that strayed away from civilization; Many changes took place on Earth. Africa was named Africa to divide black people and make them think they are different from other blacks; Blacks were formerly known as Asiactics. One slave-trader that came among the original people (Black) was named John Hawkins (Christian), he portrayed himself as a good guy and told the Asiactics that there was a new land where gold was just laying on the ground, and that he would take them in his ship, (Which was named the good ship Jesus) once they were tricked over to America and could not return 9,000 miles back home, they eventually made a song called; You can have this old world, but just give me Jesus, (The Ship). These people native tongue was Arabic, and they were cultured and refined. They came from a civilized society which built the Pyramids; which the Europeans had never seen until allowed to visit the Middle East. Even today, in many areas, Europeans need a special permit to travel and trade in the East. It can easily be argued that BLACK people was gullible but these people were not used to tricks and lies. The lived a life of honesty and their word was their Bond. (Before Mankind was loosed out of the Caves of Europe and mingled with all societies of the earth; A man's word was his bond. i.e. life).

The idea of the Europeans was to make a new man, remember Genesis 1:26–27 Let us make Man in our Image, and after our likeness. The did not just want a physical slave, they wanted a complete new man that they made in their image. (Just as they were made in the image of another man). First, they took the off-springs of the original people that were kidnapped (The first people were kidnapped; then later, some came looking for gold) and these newborns were psychologically, mentally, and spiritually killed with lies about their History, Culture, God, Language and Heritage. To the extent, that they were given new Names (So called Negroes) meaning that they were dead to the knowledge of who they were (Negro has nothing to do with a river). It means dead, or insensitive, something hard, or blind, deaf and dumb to yourself. Once dead to self, the negroes were counted as part of the livestock, and sold as part of the European's sheeps or cattle. Now if this is not A New Man (So called Negro), then what is a new man? And that is why it will take another man like the first Jesus, to save this poor soul. The Second Jesus must re-teach this Negro altogether; he must be taught his own God, Who He Is, (He has been taught that he was found swinging on limbs and came from a monkey) This is not true, it has been established already about the monkeys; Just notice what Race loves Monkeys the most! (White people).

One thing should be clear before introducing Prophet Muhammad and Fard Muhammad "The Second Coming of Jesus" and that is; THE SO CALLED NEGROES ARE THE LOST SHEEPS IN THE HOUSE OF ISRAEL AS DESCRIBED IN MATTHEW 10:6.

CHAPTER IV
Whiteman's Tricknology— The Beginning of the Blackman's Stolen Birthright in America!

Approximately 600 years after the death of Jesus Christ, another major prophet was born. His birth was following the lineage of Ishmael (remember, he was Abraham's other son that was cast out for mocking Sarah) and the name of this prophet was Muhammad Ibin Abudullah, and it was through him that the Religion of Islam emerged and started the process of revealing the truth about the Children of Israel and how they came into world domination. The Book or Scripture that each prophet received was: Moses received the Torah, Jesus received the Injil or Gospel, and Muhammad received the Holy Quran over a twenty three years period.

Muhammad was born into the leading tribe of Mecca, Arabia, and his name means "One worthy of Praise". His early life was shrouded in tragedy, for his father died a few days before he was born, his mother before he was six, so he was raised by his uncle. His own condition, developed within a love for the unfortunate, oppressed, or downtrodden, and he always wanted to better their condition in life. This character earned him the name of "The Upright". In Mecca, there were many Gods, but one God stood out from all the rest as the supreme creator. Muhammad used to wander in the desert and sit in a certain cave and meditate. Even though, he was concerned for people, he remained removed from them in outlook and ways. As he grew from childhood to manhood, the lawlessness of the tribes, the frequent quarrels, immorality, and cynicism produced into his spirit a disgust for that way of life of his people.

Upon maturity he entered the caravan business, and at the age of 25 he entered the service of a wealthy widow named Khadija. Although she was 15 years his senior, they were married. The marriage was happy and during the long years that await Muhammad of suffering and heartaches, it would be Khadija to comfort and console him. She made his burden light! It was fifteen year of preparation and spiritual communion with God before his ministry began. He was 40 years old!

Islam has five principles of beliefs. The most essential of them all is;

(1) The Belief in One God, whose proper name is Allah!
(2) The Belief in all the Prophets (Abraham, Moses, Jesus, David, Solomon) and the Truth or Revelations) that they brought to the people.
(3) Charity in all its forms; material was well as spiritual
(4) Prayer and fasting
(5) Hajj; a pilgrimage to Mecca to visit the Kabba once in the lifetime of a Muslim.

Now that we have established who the Children of Israel are; and that they are from the seed of Isaac, then who is that seed of Abraham from which the Bible spoke about in Genesis 15:12-15 Know of a surety that thy seed shall be a stranger in a land that is not their, and shall serve them; and they shall afflict them for four hundred years; And also that nation, whom they shall serve, will I judge; and afterward shall they come out with great substance. This seed of Abraham comes from Ishmael, Muhammad, and his lineage. This lineage of Abraham (Ishmael, Esau, Muhammad, was the seed that was kidnapped by the Gentiles

"Children of Israel") and made slaves in a nation that is not their. During this time the European nations were not fully developed, but when Christopher Columbus discovered the "new lands" the Europeans started looking for fresh labor to pioneer their new "nation" and thus the first people made to work the land were Muslims, and not slaves!

Prophet Muhammad explained many of the teachings of Moses and Jesus. Jesus said to Love your neighbor, but he does not make it clear as to who is our neighbor that we should love as our self, while enemies can live next door, as well as in our house. Islam makes a distinction that a believer is the brother of a believer. A Muslim believes in one God; and not set-up a son as his equal. A muslim does not believe in a three-head God; nor did Jesus. Abraham could not be the father of such a religion because he came before the Children of Israel crawled out of the cave and developed such a belief. Muhammad cleared up these misconceptions and taught the right religion which is Islam!

Islam is Man's True Religion

The primary significance about the life of Muhammad was not the fact that he established the Religion of Islam; but through him was revealed the Holy Quran. The Holy Quran is the truth that the world has been waiting for in order to understand why there is so much murdering and destroying of the nations of the earth. That is why Muhammad was at war with Cain; which is another name that the Bible symbolically uses to describe how the Children of Israel rose up and slew their brother (Abel or Ishmaelites) the world over. Remember, after being banished into the wilderness for two-thousand years, it took Moses to raise or make this new man that God promised would rule and when he was released from the hills and caves, his identity (Cain, Children of Israel, Adam and Eve) was unknown to the populace and Allah revealed it to his Prophet; i.e. Muhammad Ibin Abullah, through the Holy Quran.

All prophets have a special dispensation given to them, and Muhammad's was that the final knowledge of who each nation of people were would become known. This knowledge would let each people (nation) know what area belong to them and establish the boundaries of the land, culture, religion and all other area that determines a civilization. As previouly stated, Muhammad drove the Children of Israel (Cain) out of the East and into the West. They changed the caves and hillsides of Europe into beautiful cities and towns. They built factories making everything essential for their comforts. They became the most richest and powerful people on earth. But, keep in mind that this is for only 6,000 years, because they will not obey the laws of Allah, as predicted of them by Moses at his death. A nation's permanent success depends on its obedience to the laws of Allah (God).

Before this people came about, there were many civilizations that built the Pyramids and Sphinxs, and the modern sciences of today are based on the knowledge of yesterday. Now, we come to the last four hundred years history this 6,000 year period of the Children of Israel. The first thing is to identify the Children of Israel today with their modern names. United States, Great Britain, France, Germany, Italy, Ireland, Scotland, Scandanavian Countries or basically all European Countries including the United States and Israel, via Jacob.

Gold is Lying on the Ground in the "New World" (America)

In 1492, Christopher Columbus discovered the "new world" along with the Indians, who had been exiled on the land from India for thousands of years. The powers of England decided that they would need man-power to develop the new world so they commissioned slave-traders like John Hawkins to come among the people of the East (Muslims) and buy, borrow, or steal the necessary people for this work. John Hawkins had a ship named the "Good Ship Jesus" and he fooled the first muslims (Black People) over here by lying; promising that they could come over here and get a sack of gold easily because it was just lying on the ground, and return home. They did no know that the intentions of the Children of Israel was to put them in slavery. A few came over with the trader; he did not buy slaves, they were made slaves once they landed on the soil of America in 1555. (Immigrants are still falling for that trick; there is gold on the streets of America, let us go there and get all we want and return home.

The Making of a Negro

The first muslims (Blacks) landed in America in 1555, and they did not come out of the jungles of Africa, but from Egypt land, down on the River of Nile. They were not savages (uncivilized) when they came here, but were made savages (uncivilized) when they got here; Here is how it was done! The first muslims (Blacks) could not speak any English, because their native tongue was Arabic. They knew their God (Allah) and their culture (Islam), they knew the sciences of Mathematics, Astronomy, Irrigation, and other sciences of building a nation. So they used their brain-power to develop the nation and they took their off-springs and would not let the muslims raise their children. The (Gentiles) refuse to educate the black children (muslims) in any ways of being himself or anything true about himself. They (off-springs) were mis-educated or taught falsely about their Heritage, Culture and their God. They were taught that the Gentiles were their benefactors because they were found swinging on trees in Africa, In order words they used their own history and mental birth control to make the blacks of America blind, deaf, and dumb to his own self. This condition of being brain-washed was accepted by the children, and they had children until after a period of 64 years, there were a group of people in America who did not know where they came from, who they were, or anything about the planet on which they they lived; totally blind, deaf, and dumb to the knowledge of self. This condition is still prevalent today!

Now, they (Gentiles or Children of Israel) not only mis-educated the muslims (blacks) but they gave them a new education; it is called A Negro's Education or today Negro History. The word negro means "dead" or neutral, or something to be moved, and when the Mind of the muslims (blacks) had become neutralized or dead to who they were, then they were called Negroes! The history books say that the Black Man of America came here negroes in 1619, and that is not true because it hides the 64 years in which the Muslims were made Negroes in America. Remember, whether muslim or negro, this is still the seed of Abraham that will come out from among these strangers with great substance. THIS IS HOW THE BLACKMAN'S BIRTHRIGHT (Mental Birth Control) WAS STOLEN!

History Repeats Itself: Blacks Exiled in America!

In 1619, the beginning of a new era of organized slavery took place within the new world, and this lasted until after the Civil War (1861-1865) when legalized slavery was abolished. But the education of slavery and the lack of knowledge as to who the slave really was had been internalized by the slave. He had become a mental cripple to his master, and unable to provide for himself because the Gentiles did not re-educate the slave into the ways of a free and civilized man. Therefore, he was tricked again into thinking that he was free, when he was still tied to the Mind of this captors; In order to be completely free, he would need the knowledge of his own way of life, culture, and God. In order to receive this knowledge he would need a new Moses to Resurrect him from this Dead State of Mind and the slave's master was not about to re-educate him because a man that will not "treat" you right, most certainly will not "teach" you right! The next major step in the "Resurrection of the Dead" (Negro) was that the slave had taken the Name, Religion, History, and the characteristics of his master.

This process of the slave identifying himself so much with his captors that he forgets that he is captured is common today in terrorism, and a de-briefing process in necessary before the captor can be re-united with his own kind. Well, this is what is needed with the Negro's mind. In 1930, a major incident happened in America. The Christian world has been looking for the return of Jesus Christ to save the world. But, the man that came on the scene was named Fard Muhammad (Muslim) and he preached the Resurrection of the Dead for the so-called American Negroes. He described everything about the people on earth and said that he was the Jesus that the world had been looking for (Believe it or not).

He left a Moses for the negroes in the person of the Hon. Elijah Muhammad and this man (Elijah Muhammad) established the Nation of Islam to act as a training vehicle to re-educate the negroes back into the knowledge of themselves. This re-education process going on among the negroes of America is known as the Resurrection of the Dead. It is a Spiritual Resurrection! Both these men have left the scene just like Moses and Jesus, but the teachings and the on-going process remain and will never stop until every slave wake-up and realize his identity and Be Himself! A Muslim! But, being realistic, no one changes unless they are made uncomfortable and at the present time, the slave is very comfortable being a slave so why worry about being a Muslim. The point is that God (Allah) wants every nation and people to return to their own ways of life and Money system. (Including this Negro; Seed of Abraham).

For the past 6,000 years the world has been living according to the Money System of the Children of Israel and their time is up to rule the planet according to their ways and habits. The fighting that is taking place all over the world is a result of a change in world rulership. The Gentiles are not giving up this power and glory without a fight. But it is futile, because what ever the "Will of God" is going to be, then, that is what's going to be! The wheels have been set in motion since 1914, and we are not witnessing the end of a world, but rather the beginning of a new one, so sit back and enjoy each step of this journey called the "Resurrection of the Dead."

CHAPTER V
Master Fard Muhammad is the God that came to RESTORE the Blackman's Birthright

History of Master Fard Muhammad

The Second Jesus, is our Saviour, i.e., Fard Muhammad was born February 26, 1877 in Mecca, Arabia. His father was a black man and his mother was Jewish. His father planned his birth this way of mixed (Black and White) parentage, because he was born for a special purpose in life.i.e. that of Resurrecting a Dead Humanity back to Spiritual Life. This is the man that Jesus Christ (Essau Ibin Yusef) spoke of in John 15:26 wherein he said: But when the Comforter is come, whom I will send unto you from the Father, even the Spirit of truth, who preceedeth from the Father, he shall testify of me.

The name Fard means "Early Morning" and Muhammad means "Praiseworthy" thus we have one coming in the Early Morning of the seventh thousand year that is worthy of Praise to bring about a complete change in the world. First, let us review how religious scripture is passed on from person to person. In terms of God, there is always "One" that has access to the Divine Scripture of the people. There have always been national prophets commissioned or transmitting the scriptures from time to time like Daniel, Isiah, or Jesus.

However, the God is not necessarily a man on a throne like a king, but rather the knowledge of WHO IS

Master Fard Muhammad born February 26, 1877

GOD is passed on from time immemorial from God to God, down to the father of Fard Muhammad on to the Son, which is our Saviour today, the Second Jesus, God in Person, Master Fard Muhammad. He was "Born" for this work of Resurrecting the Dead, and although he went to schools, the schools did not prepare him for his mission. His father taught him the History of the Universe, the Creation of Man, History of the Blackman and Whiteman, the knowledge of God and the Devil. How the Devil was made. The correct meaning of Scripture. How the world became confused over Heaven and Hell. His job was to put the Blackman (Righteous Blackman) back in his rightful position of authority by teaching him a thorough knowledge of himself.

His purpose was to re-establish the Kingdom of God on earth as it was before the making of the Devil; all those who refuse to accept righteousness will be destroyed during this transition or change of worlds.

World Traveler

He spent 42 years preparing himself for his purpose of Resurrecting the Dead. He traveled to the United States, and was in and out for many years. He waited until the Stock Market Crash of 1929 before he made his announcement of who he was in 1930. Matthew 24: 42–44 Bible states, He comes as a thief in the night. He stated that he was God in Person, that the Blackman was asleep to his real identity (God) and the Whiteman. He announced That the world has been mislead about the true and correct interpretation of the scriptures. That a change in world-economic power was taking place, and that a wise person need only watch and see the Money-System being revised.

A final clarification on Master Fard Muhammad being God or God in Person. Man is the Supreme Being. The Supreme Being is God. The Universal Power within creation that manifested this Universes and Man is called Allah. God means power and force and is a Spiritual term used to identify the Divine Power that's resident in Man's Mind. When a Man appears on the scene proclaiming that he is God (He Is Telling The Truth) although his purpose is to awaken the population to their own Divinity as being Gods of the earth.

To understand Master Fard Muhammad "Spiritually" is to finally understand YOURSELF, and your Divine Origin. This truth should make Man (Blackman) See himself as God and not the Slave-Image that he has accepted as himself. To conclude, Master Fard Muhammad is a friend to the Blackman and Woman of America and is fulfilling Scripture like Jesus of 2,000 years ago. He is not interested in you accepting him as God but rather Seeing Yourself As God, so that you can fulfill your destiny as a Chosen People.

The True Spiritual-Image of Master Fard Muhammad is God, and the True Spiritual-Image of the Blackman is God, There is no difference! One is in the knowledge of himself and the other is Blind, Deaf and Dumb. Master Fard Muhammad comes to teach the Blackman WHO HE IS!!

Reality of God and the Devil

Matthew 24: 42–44 Watch, therefore; for ye know not what hour your Lord doth come. 43 But know this, that if the /householder/ had known in what watch the thief would come, he would have watched, and would not have /allowed/ his house to be broken /into/. 44 Therefore be ye also ready; for as in such an hour as ye think not the Son of Man cometh. It was in the very darkest hour of Depression for the United States that the Second Jesus (Master Fard Muhammad) made himself known publicly for the first time as to his real identity. The Son of Man or Second Jesus that was prophecied in the Bible. He made this earth-shattering announcement not on the radio but in a public meeting for blacks (ex-slaves) in Detroit, MI. on July 4, 1930. Naturally, the world was not listening!

What is it besides Scripture that indicates that this man is the return of Jesus? First he comes at the end of Satan's rule over the earth's population, and set-up a new pattern of living that will remove sickness and disease. He reveals how the Blackman and woman's history and how they became physical slaves and are now in mental and spiritual slavery. He explains how our Names, Culture, and Religion was taken and replaced with the Devil's Names, Culture and Religion. He explains how the Whiteman's Economics and for the past 6,000 years have ruled the world in unrighteousness. He explains that our return to practicing righteousness is our only salvation and Islam was given to us as a Religion.

Not the old orthodox Islam, but a new Islam that enables you to see the God within yourself. There is no God in the sky nor Devil in the ground; God and the Devil dwells within people both Black and White! However, the Blackman was created from black mud fashioned into shape, and the Whiteman from intense hot fire. What makes the Blackman complete is that he will accept God's Divine Spirit and follow his laws, wherein the Whiteman will not, thus making him alien in the eye-sight of God and the Righteous. That is the true meaning of God and the Devil; who will or will not accept the Spirit of God and follow his commandments, it makes no difference to God whether you are Black and White.

The Coming of The Second Jesus

Jesus (Master Fard Muhammad) comes at the end of Satan's time to rule over the earth. He appeared on July 4, 1930 and announced that the the Resurrection of the Dead had begun world-wide but especially here in America among the So-Called Negroes because they had been poisoned the most by being reared up in the house of the Devil. The Resurrection has three stages to it; i.e. the first stage is the Animal stage or self-accusing spirit, the second stage is the human stage, and the third stage is the Divine or God in man. The Resurrection is designed to bring about the "rising of humanity" to a *Godly level of living* instead of the *Animal level of living* currently practiced by Mankind.

Master Fard Muhammad was born for this mission on February 26, 1877. He spent forty-two years of his life preparing for this mission of "Raising the Consciousness" of humanity, to a Divine level. His primary goal of raising the dead is written in the Bible in Luke 16:19–31, of Lazarus and the Rich Man; And his overall goal is to re-establish Righteousness on the earth. The Resurrection is taken from Chapter 75 of the Holy Quran. He must raise the sleeping dead Lazarus (So-Called Negroes) to life with Truth. Lazarus is dead in a shallow (mental grave) that only needs shaking, with Divine Truth. However, he must BELIEVE and PRACTICE this truth in order to come alive. He (Lazarus) has been deprived of his own wisdom and knowledge for almost 400 years, and have been totally remade in the image of his enemy (whiteman), and now have a new identity (Negro) within the devil's culture. Negro means one that is dead to his own culture (Blackman).

Thus the scripture was fulfilled wherein it says John 1:11 He came unto his own, and his own received him not. The So-Called Negroes rejected Master Fard Muhammad's teachings because they could not recognize him for who he really was (God). This was due to how they had been re-made in accordance with a "slave's mentality" and as a result of what was done to the Negroes, Allah charged the American White People (America) as being the most wicked people on earth, and would be the first to be destroyed in the Judgement.

Fard Muhammad (God in Person) began teaching Islam to the So-Called Negroes of America. He taught that the Blackman was the first man on earth and was destined to be the last, if there is a last. That the So-Called Negroes were not Negroes but rather were the Seed of Abraham that had been lost for over 400 years among strange people, and had been abused and mistreated beyond recognition as the Poeple of God. The strangers that were responsible for this mistreatment were European White People. He taught that it is now time for the So-Called Negroes to build a Nation for themselves, Genesis 15 13–14. Because of there trials, they have been chosen to lead the other nations in Righteousness, with God's (Master Fard Muhammad) unlimited wisdom and knowledge. Revelation 21:3 And I heard a great voice out of heaven saying, Behold, the tabernacle of God is with men, and he will dwell with them, and they shall be his people, and God himself shall be with them, and be their God. The nation that the negroes will build will be a Muslim Nation with New wisdom from the old previous ways of orthodox Islam. God makes All Things New! Rev. 21:5

The Birth of A New Muslim Nation from the So-Called Negroes may seem difficult to accept at first hand, but when they are cleaned up morally, spiritually and in their proper garments, then the world will bear witness that these are the People of God. They can't be judged as God's people now because they are not themselves. That is why, the Coming of God is known spiritually as the "Resurrection of the Dead". The dead must be raised before the world (White World) can be judged according to their deeds. The scripture describes it this way in Luke 16:19–31 Lazarus and the Rich Man.

19 There was a certain rich man, who was clothed in purple and fine linen, and fared sumptuously every day. 20 And there was certain beggar, named Lazarus, who was laid at his gate full of sores. 22 And it came to pass that the beggar died, and was carried by the angels into Abraham's bosom; the rich man also died, and was buried; 23 And in

hell he lifted up his eyes, being in tormets and seeth Abraham afar off, and Lazarus in his bosom.

The meaning of this parable is as follows; the So-Called Negroes (Lazarus) have suffered as a beggar in America and as a result of this mistreatment and suffering has "died as a self-sufficient people". The Rich Man (White Man of America) has eaten sumptuously every day in every conceivable way and mistreated this poor beggar. He died also, "lost his wealth and world power due to the way he mis-used people all over the world. The rich man (in hell) saw Lazarus in the bosom of Abraham (Protection of God) and cried out for help for him and his five brethren (Europeans), however God (Abraham) said that they (Europeans have Moses and the prophets for 6,000 years, and if they did not hear them, then surely they will not do right even if one rose from the dead like Lazarus. Lazarus (So-Called Negroes) went on to build a great nation of everlasting-righteousness.

Master Fard Muhammad is also that Jesus of the Bible in John 11:11–44 These thing said he; and after that he saith unto them, Our friend Lazarus sleepeth; but I go, that I may awake him out of sleep. 14. Then Jesus said unto them plainly, Lazarus is dead. 17 Then when Jesus came he found that he had laid in the grave four days already (four hundred years). 24 Martha said that I know that he shall rise again in the resurrection at the last day. 41 Then they took away the stone (False Doctrine of Christianity) from the place where the dead was laid. 44 and he that was dead (mental and spiritual) came forth, bound hand and foot with graveclothes; and his face was bound with a cloth (blind, deaf, and dumb to Truth) Jesus said unto them, Loose him, and let him go.

The meaning is clear that Lazarus (So-Called Negroes) were made blind, deaf, and dumb, and eventually died Spiritually and Mentally from being taught and fed mental poison (Christianity) in America. The removal of this *stone* from the minds of the Negroes will give them mental life (Islam) again and thus fulfill the prophecy of the Resurrection of the Dead.

Master Fard Muhammad gives "Understanding" of the Scriptures

Once the "stone" (christianity) has been removed from the mind of Lazarus (So-Called Negroes), then and only then can the true understanding and meaning of vital scriptural terms be applied to their lives. Let us begin with the true meaning of Heaven and Hell. Christianity teaches that heaven is in the sky and you go there after you die to meet your Lord. Hell is in the ground and you go there after you die, only to be punished forever and ever for your sins on earth. These teachings were interpreted by Europeans (white people) who operates Christianity and the Father is the Pope of Rome Another Whiteman while they get rich and live in luxury here on earth, because once you are dead, that is it! Now, here is the true meaning of Heaven and Hell

Heaven and Hell begins in this life. The sustenance that a righteous or evil person receive is known in this world. Heaven is the peace that comes from one's Soul that is at rest with God and his laws. When one's Soul is at rest with God, this is the highest spiritual bliss that one can attain in this life on earth. There is no grief, fatigue, or toil and the heart is purified of all rancor and jealousy. Peace and security reigns all around you, this is Heaven! However, this is not a place, it is essentially a state of mind, for higher and higher states of mind. It is ever-lasting as long as you are in God, and obeying his laws.

Hell is also a state of mind, and it is not meant for punishment or torture, but rather for purification, in order to make a person fit for spiritual advancement. The idea underlying hell is that whomever has wasted their opportunity to do good shall under the inevitable law which makes every man tastes of what he has done "be given another chance by undergoing a course of treatment, sometimes called a chastisement for their spiritual diseases." Individuals with a Reprobate Mind practicing such spiritual habits as Lying, Cheating, Stealing, Murdering, Envy, and Jealousy must be purified, and when God brings his punishment, it is for their benefit to change and not to their detriment.

If it were not for God ordaining a Hell for remedial purposes for purification then how could he save us? WE MUST BE PURIFIED AND MADE FIT TO ENTER THE KINGDOM OF GOD (MENTALLY).

So, Heaven and Hell are two conditions of life, and not two places that you go to after you die, but instead two conditions that you experience while you live. Nothing comes out of the sky except rain, snow, hail, or other conditions brought about through changes in the atmosphere. Another misconception that must be cleared up is Life after Death.

Life after Death

Death is a stage in Evolution. Just as from dust is evolved the man, so it is that from the deeds which he does, evolves the higher or lower man. Death is only a stage in growth or regression. As from the small life germ the man grows up, but he does not lose his individuality, although he undergoes many changes, so from this man is made the higher man. His attributes changes and he is made to grow into what he cannot conceive at the present. Each stage of growth is a form of death and growing out of that stage is a form of new life. A life after death is normally a new world of advancement and progress, and the old world become insignificant. Physical death settles all things and God did not ordain any physicall dead people (Jesus included) to come back and give instructions to the living about life or anything else. In fact, Jesus said himself "Let the dead bury the dead" meaning that his message was for the living and not dead people.

The Resurrection of the Dead is referred to as giving life to the dead, however, it only means a continuation of this present life, because these people were mentally and spiritually dead, and not physically dead. Life after being spiritually dead is God means peace and a beautiful life in righteousness. Most people are living a wicked life because of the false concepts of God that they are practicing as truths, taught to them in Christianity such as; Good and Evil, God and Devil, Hereafter, Jesus and other superstitious practices.

The Hereafter should be understood, because it does not mean that after you die, you will go to heaven or hell, but rather the Hereafter means "to be here on earth, alive, after the veil of falsehood has been removed from your mind" and you are raised up into the knowledge of God. Another meaning is to be here after the Devil has been removed from the throne of your mind as the ruling power, and replaced by God as the ruling power over your mind. That is the Hereafter, after the Devil comes god! All of this Heaven and Hell, Life after Death, and the Hereafter are conditions of life that takes place within the minds of people. Nothing takes place after one dies, when one is dead, that is it, you're done!

Now, the reason why man is so estrange from God, it is because of material greed. This civilization (America and its Allies) are so engrossed in the contest of manufacturing that they have no thought of God. A great world-conflict is going on for wealth and more wealth, and God is the only one that can restore the balance to the world. Material benefits have turned man into the enemy of man. The day of peace for this world will come about when man realizes that there is only one nation, and that is the human nation.

People (Devils) that are working against the plans of God will be brought to disgrace. Material acquisitions are fine in and of themselves, but don't neglect your soul by deceptive practices, and denying others access to God by perpetuating fasle teachings like (Jesus is alive in heaven and you will get your reward when you meet him). This is done so that the poor will seek their material reward in the sky, while the rich receive their reward her on earth while they live. It is a spiritual poisoning of the poor all over the world through Christianity. The truth of Islam will awaken the poor to their reward here on earth, during this Resurrection of the Dead, preached from the mouth of God, Master Fard Muhammad. He described the Minds of the Negroes as likened to a "frozen embryo" that only needs thawing out with the sunlight of Islam.

CHAPTER VI
The First Jesus

Jesus Christ (Esau Ibin Yusef) was a Prophet; Not a God

Jesus means Justice and Christ means Chrusher, however Jesus Christ did not come to chrush or destroy the Jews civilization of two-thousand years ago, but rather in fulfillment of the prophecy of Moses. he was a Prophet of God, and his name was Esau. Ibin Yusef means the son of Joseph. The Jews gave him the name of Christ because they said he was a troublemaker. Jesus main teachings of the Resurrection of the Dead centered around a future people and time. He had reference to his brothers and sisters that would be lost in a foreign land he described them as the Lost Sheep in the House of Israel. He described how they would be raised from the dead in the parable of Lazarus and the Rich Man. Dead means unaware of God's Consciousness within.

The Lost Sheeps (So-Called Negroes) were stripped of their identity by an enemy (White people) and given the name Negro. It is a mental and spiritual condition that can be eliminated by practicing their own way of life; Islam. Jesus said that God would send them a comforter and that when he returned (Master Fard Muhammad is the second Jesus in Spirit), he would eliminate all their ills. The comforter is Master Fard Muhammad, who has established the Nation of Islam to remove the stigma of being called Negroes by teaching what Negro means and how to remove it from the minds.

Remember, Negro means Dead. It means that the Black Man has a dead state of mind when it comes to himself and kind. It means that he does not know his true History, Culture, Religion, God, or Way of Life. It means that he is still a slave to the whiteman's Economy, Religion, Culture, God, and Way of Life. Again, a Negro is a mental and spiritual state of mind that is dead to itself and kind. God and his Messenger, Hon. Elijah Muhammad has provided a way to correct this condition if the Blackman would only accept Islam, and practice it as his original way of life. Islam will cure his spiritual and mental ills by teaching him who he is. Because being a Negro is a state of mind and not a nationality, the Blackman will be resurrected over a period of time, but many will not be saved because of disbelief.

Jesus (Ibn Yusef) Taught Love Thy Neighbor as Thyself

Jesus spoke in parables, symbolism and metaphors and one day his disciples said unto him, why speakest thou unto them in parables? Matthew 13:10–11 He answered and said on to them, Because it is given unto you to know the mysteries of the Kingdom of Heaven, but to them it is not given. The hour that Jesus spoke about was the end of the time that this world of evil was given to rule over Mankind; 6,000 years! The dead that would rise; would be the spitirually dead people that had been killed by falsehood, lies, and misunderstandings, and they would hear the truth and be resurrected spiritually and live. In the last days, all the graves (Nations) shall hear his voice (The second Jesus) and come forth to life or to damnation because of the evil that they have done. The Dead that would rise is the mentally dead negroes of America. Negro means Dead.

For an historical perspective, (Adam and Eve) to a present or future outlook the subject will refer to Adam and Eve as White People their current identity is all *Euro-*

pean Nations that have spread out all over the planet. Later this global identity will evolve into two distinct separate world powers, and these two powers control the world today! White People or the European Nations have dominated the whole world and thus fulfilled the prophecy of bringing the world into subjection. However at the end of time (1914) the Bible makes it clear that the nation rising up against nation is to the European conflicts that we have witnessed. Basically, White People have subdued the whole world, but could not agree on the division of the spoils, and they are at one another's throat and this struggle has assumed the form of a World War. One world war ends only to be followed by another. We have seen hell raging on this earth in World War II. What World War III may bring, no one can say for sure.

The Beatitudes

St Matthews 5:2 and seeing the multitudes, he went up into a mountain: and when he was set, his disciples came unto him: Remember, he *saw* the multitudes but he was talking to his disciples or followers on a mountain.

2. And he opened his mouth, and taught them, saying,
3. Blessed are the poor in spirit, for theirs is the Kingdom of Heaven.
4. Blessed are they that mourned; for they shall be comforted.
5. Blessed are the meek; for they shall inheir the earth.
6. Blessed are they who do hunger and thirst after righteousness; for they shall be filled.
7. Blessed are the merciful; for they shall obtain mercy.
8. Blessed are the pure in heart; for they shall see God.
9. Blessed are the peacemakers; for they shall be called the sons of God.
10. Blessed are they who are persecuted for righteousness sake; for theirs is the Kingdom of Heaven.

11. Blessed are ye, when men shall revile, persecute you and say all manner of evil against you falsely for my sake.
12. Rejoice, and be exceedingly glad; for great is your reward in heaven,; for so persecuted they the prophets who were before you.

The Similitudes

13. Ye are the salt of the Earth, but if the salt has lost savor, with what shall it be salted? It is thereafter good for nothing but to cast out and be trodden under foot of men.
14. Ye are the light of the world. A city that is set on a hill cannot be hidden.
15. Neither do men light a /lamp/ and put it under a bushel, but on a /lampstand/ and it giveth light unto all that are in the house.
16. Let your light so shine before me, that they may see your good works and glorify your father who is in heaven.

Relation of Christ to the Law

17. *Think not that I am come to destroy the law (of Moses) or the prophets I am not come to destroy, but to fulfill.*
18. For verily I say unto you, Till heaven and earth pass, one jot or one tittle shall in no way pass from the law, till all be fulfilled.
19. Whosoever, therefore, shall break one of these least commandments, and shall teach men so, he shall be called the least in the Kingdom of Heaven; but whosoever shall do and teach them, the same shall be called great in the Kingdon of Heaven.
20. For I say unto you that except your righteousness shall exceed the righteousness of the Scribes and Pharisees, ye shall in no case enter into the Kingdom of Heaven.

First Reconciliation, then Sacrifice

21. Ye have heard that it was said by them of old, Thou shall not kill and whosoever shall kill shall be in danger of the judgement.
22. But I say unto you that whosoever is angry with his brother without a cause shall be in danger of judgement; and whosoever shall say to his brother, Ra ca, shall be in danger of the council; but whosoever shall say thou fool, shall be in danger of hell fire.
23. Therefore, if thou bring thou gift to the altar and there rememberest that thy brother hath anything against thee.
24. Leave there thy gift before the altar and go thy way; first be reconciled, to thy brother, and then come and offer thy gift.
25. Agree with thine adversary quickly while thy are in the way with him, lest at anytime the adversary deliver thee to the judge. and the judge deliver thee to the officer and thou be cast into prison.
26. Verily I say unto thee, Thou shall be no means come out from there till thou has paid the utmost farthing.

Lust, Adultery and Divorce

27. Ye have heard that it was said by them of old, Thou shall not commit Adultery.
28. But I say unto you that whosoever looketh on a woman to lust after her hath committed adultery with her in his heart.
29. And if thy right eye offend thee, pluck it out and cast it from thee; for it is profitable for thee that one of thy members should perish, and not that thy whole body should be cast into hell.
30. And if thy right hand offend thee, cut it off and cast it from thee; for it is profitable for thee that one of thy members should perish and not that thy whole body should be cast into hell.

31. It has been said, whosoever shall put away his wife, let him give her a writing divorcement.
32. But I say unto you that whosoever shall put away his wife, /except/ for the cause of fornication causeth her to commit adultery; and whosoever shall marry her that is divorced committeth adultery.

Perjury and Retaliation Forbidden

33. Again, ye have heard it hath been said by them of old, Thou shall not /perjure/ thyself, but shall perform unto the Lord thine oaths.
34. But, I say unto you, swear not at all; neither by heaven, for it is God's throne.
35. Nor by the earth, for it is his footstool, neither by Jerusalem, for it is the city of the great king.
36. Neither shall thou swear by head, because thou canst not make one hair white or black.
37. But let your communication be, Yea, Yea; Nay, Nay; for whatever is more than these cometh of evil.
38. Ye have heard that it hath been said, an eye for an eye, and a tooth for a tooth.
39. But I say unto you that you resist not evil, but whosoever shall smite thee on they right cheek, turn to him the other also.
40. And if any man will sue thee at the law, and take away thy coat, let him have thy cloak also.
41. And whosoever shall compel thee to go a mile go with him /two/.
42. Give to him that asketh thee, and from him that would borrow of thee turn not thou away.

Love of Enemies Enjoined

43. Ye have heard that it hath been said, Thou shall love neighbor and hate thine enemies.

44. But I say unto you, Love your enemies, bless them that curse, do good to them that hate you, and pray for them that despitefully use you and persecute.
45. That ye may be the /sons/ of your father, who is in heaven; for he maketh his son to shine on the evil and on the good, and sendeth rain on the just and the unjust.
46. For if you love them who love you, what reward have ye? Do not even the /tax collectors/ the same?
47. And if ye /greet/ your brethren only, What do ye more than others? Do not even the /heathens/ so?
48. Be ye, therefore perfect, even as your father, who is in heaven, is perfect.

Jesus constant cry was "I come not to destroy the law but to fulfill it." To fulfill means to be in actuality. The authorities chased Jesus until he became discouraging to them. They named him Christ (which means trouble-maker) because every time they would get there, he would be gone. Jesus taught twenty-two years on the run. Until, at last he read and understood that he was too soon; TWO THOUSAND YEARS TOO SOON! The next Jesus (Fard Muhammad) will raise the dead So-Called Negroes of America. Raise them to a "New Moral System built by—themselves."

CHAPTER VII
The Dwellers In The Cave

The Dwellers of the Cave for 375 years Is a Lost People

I mentioned earlier that God had an alternate plan for the uplift-of the So-Called Negroes in America. The plan is called Islam or Divine Revelation. Approximately six-hundred years after the death of Jesus Christ, another major prophet was born in the Holy City of Mecca, Arabia and his name was Muhammad Ibin Abdullah. In the last six-thousand years there have been four major prophets and three were given scriptures for this world to be guided by; Abraham was promised that his seed would inherit the Kingdom of God, Moses received the Torah or scriptures for Judaism, and Jesus received the Injil or Gospel for the Christians, and Prophet Muhammad received the Holy Quran for the Muslims over a period of twenty-three years. Now, none of these prophets understood fully the scriptures that they received from God during their lifetimes, nor was all of these scriptures to be fulfilled until the end of this time for the Devil to rule the earth, which was six-thousand years.

At the end of this six-thousand year period, God made his appearance in the world in the person of Master Fard Muhammad in 1930. (Just as God made his appearance in the other prophets like Moses, Jesus or Muhammad), He raised up (mental and spiritual) a Messenger, i.e. Elijah Muhammad to teach and explain all of the scriptures from every prophet and every book, and let the world know Who the Whiteman is? Who the Blackman is? What time it is and that the first thing that must be accomplished is the So-Called Negroes must be raised up and put back on their feet as a nation. Now, let us study the Holy Quran and find out who were the Dwellers in the Cave for 375 years.

Chapter 18, verse 11 and 12 of Holy Quran, section 2: reads as follows. 11 So we prevented them from hearing in the cave for a number of years. 12. Then we raised them up that we might know which of the two parties was best able to calculate the time for which they remained. 1482 The preventing from hearing is understood to be the equivalent to causing to sleep (mental sleep). but the original meaning is favoured by the context, the significance being that these people remained cut off from the rest of the world for a number of years. 1482a The "raising them up" might siginfy raising them up from sleep, as also raising them up into a condition of activity, after their remaining cut off from the world. 1483 attempts to identify these dwellers of the Cave and their whereabouts by stating it this way. There is another plausible suggestion that the person referred to were Joseph of Arimathaea and some early Christians, their place of refuge being Glastonbury in England, which on account of it northern position well answers the description of the Cave. Gibbon states that these people remained in this condition for 375 years. Now, the explanation to this story in the Holy Quran.

The people that were put in the Cave for 375 years were not Joseph of Arimathaea, but Joseph of Egypt or the Blackman from the East or So-Called Negroes, the Cave was not Glastonbury England but a colony of England the United States of America. From the time of enslavement in the Cave of America, 1555, to the time of the coming of God, 1930, (Master Fard Muhammad) was exactly 375 years. It was at that time that he announced that the So-Called Negroes was to wake up from their long mental sleep and build a nation of their own. He gave them the Sun, Moon and Stars as their Flag thus fulfilling Joseph dream (at least one part of it), the second part of the dream of rising up as a ruler within the government of Pharaoh will take place but in his own government; i.e. Nation of Islam.

The destiny of the Blackman is in his own nation and not as a slave within the whiteman's government. The fight today is for the slave to understand just who he is dealing with and why God said Build Your Own Money-System, Education, or I should say the proper Spiritual education is what the blackman is lacking, so God has given the Blackman and Whiteman a grace period to "get right morally" during this period called the Resurrection of the Dead, before the Judgement set in, because the time for the White man to rule the world ended in 1914. A New Moral-System!

Scripture Teaches That the Whiteman Was Made to Rule For 6,000 Years!

In order to fully understand why the Blackman was kidnapped from his home, wars constantly being fought, nations fighting against nations, and generally no peace on earth, then one must understand the true identity of the whiteman. The Bible states it this way Chapter 20, verses 7 and 8. And when the thousand years are ended, Satan shall be loosed out of his prison, 8 And shall go out to deceive the nations which are in the four quarters of the earth, Gog and Magog, to gather them together to battle; the numbers of whom is as the sand of the sea.

The Holy Quran states this in Chapter 18 verse 94. They said: O *Dhu*-l-qarnain, Gog and Magog do mischief in the land. May we then pay thee tribute on condition that thou raise a barrier between us and them? 1523 This verse brings us face to face with the all important subject, viz., the identity of Gog and Magog. We are told that Gog and Magog will again be let loose in the later days. When Gog and Magog are let loose they will sally forth from every point of eminence, and they will dominate the whole world. "They will drink the water of the whole world," the ancestors of Gog and Magog are the Slav and Teutonic races, and in the world domination of Gog and Magog is thus clearly hinted the domination of the "European nations" over the whole world, and the prophecy has thus found fulfillment in our days. The Quran makes it clear that Gog and Magog is none other than the European Nations or White People.

The "letting loose on the world" was their leaving the confinement of Europe and causing nations to fight against nations. The Bible describes Satan as Gog and Magog let loose on the world, and the Holy Quran identifies Gog and Magog as the Europeans let loose on the world; Thus the conclusion is that Satan is the Europeans (White people) or commonly expressed as "The Whiteman is the Devil. Now, the Devil was given 6,000 years to rule the earth, and then God (Blackman) would take over again. We are in that that transition period in history wherein the world is going back to the rightful owners (Blackman and his kind).

But first, let us go back to the Holy Quran, Chapter 2 Section 4, verse 30 titled; Greatness of Man and Need of Revelation. And when thy Lord said to the angels, I am going to place a ruler in the earth, they said: Wilt thou place in it such as make mischief in it and shed blood? And we celebrate Thy praise and extol Thy holiness. He said: Surely I know what you know not. God's purpose with Man is to make him perfect and in order to do that he had to show Man the evil that was within himself so that he could Conquer Self. God made iblis, Devil or Whiteman the opposite of the Man (Blackman). Iblis stands for the lower desires which keeps Man off the path of righteousness. (The devil's purpose to reveal Man to himself).

In the Garden, Man was instructed to stay away from the tree of immortality, tree of death, tree of sin or the tree of evil. It is evil that man is warned again and again to stay away from, and it is evil that all prophets of God have warned men about. Man is entitled to all of the benefits of nature as long as he does not forget his soul. Sin destroys his soul. Here is how the Devil brought down Man from Grace. He cast an evil suggestion in the minds of both Blackman and Woman that he would make manifest to them things that were hidden. (Their low desires)!

The devil goes around the planet sowing evil suggestions in the hearts of men and women and they are too weak to resist. Man is too weak to over come the evil suggestions of the Devil, or the evil inclination in himself. So God comes and reveals himself (Fard MUhammad) to man. He gives Revelation which strengthens Man Faith in God and gives him the strength to resist the Devil and reject his suggestions. It is by following the Guidance sent by God through his prophets that man will attain to perfection. The Devil was made as a "tool for drawing out man's evil inclination to the surface." Man's state of perfection is; There is no fear, nor grief, because man's devil has been subjugated and he now turns his life to its best use.

The outside Devil, Satan, or Whiteman is only a manifestation of what is inside the blackman (evil inclinations) and can be controlled with Divine Revelation and practicing God's Way of Life (Islam).

In order for Man to truly know himself and attain to his perfection greatness, God has established a two-way method of knowing something. First, God makes a creature, human, or plant to study in real or physical life. Second, he gives you Divine Revelation or knowledge to correlate with the physical fact of life. If one cannot accept these two as one, the it is because the individual does not want to accept the facts.

God made this world for six-thousand years and gave this people (White-people) control over it for that period of time, it is now up! The black man and woman must have their home back; i.e. earth. Master Fard Muhammad (Supreme Being) is in the world putting everthing back in its place. The War of Armageddon is on and the changes are in motion all over the earth. The balance of the time during the nineties will be very dramatic in deed.

Remember, the two makes one; Physically, the devil is in the world and everyone can see it. Second, God has made his presence and given the Divine Revelation. The only thing left is to Watch as well as Pray! Once the world of the Black man wakes up to who the Devil really is, then God will put it in their hearts to shun them. This is a repeat of how it was in the beginning of their existence. When they were first made on Patmos and came back to to the mainland among the original (black) people, the public did not know the nature in which white people were made (evil and mischevious).

Once among the black people for six months, they made so much trouble by lying and causing confusion among the people that the government officials had them all rounded up (most of them) and stripped them of all clothing, (except a loin cloth to hide their nakedness), literature, and other necessities to start a civilization. They were marched across the Arabian Desert to the hills and caves of Europe, where they lived a Caveman's life for two thousand years as punishment for breaking the Laws of God and causing mischief The first punishment was mental and spiritual (Confinement in the caves), the second punishment is the final Judgement is total destruction as a people to rule over the earth. They have been judged by God and found wanting! Rev. 20:10 And the Devil that deceived them was cast into a lake of fire and brimstone.

Gog and Magog

From a modern perspective to a future outlook, the subject (Gog and Magog) refers to America and Russia or

USA and USSR. Their overall identity is all European Nations that have spread all over the world and evolve into two distinct separate world powers, and these two powers control the world today. The 6,000 years given to this world to rule over Man by Mankind was over in 1914, and since that time, the world has been going through a "changing of the guards" from the rule of Satan to the rule of God. Let me say this; the color of a person's skin has nothing to do with God' righteousness during this period of "cleaning up". During this grace period given by God to spiritually cleanse oneself and be made fit for the Kingdom of God, if they do not clean up (black or White) then the Judgement will set in. (You will be destroyed by your own lifestyle).

The purpose of God's coming is to separate the righteous from the unrighteous. He does this separation by giving us Islam; i.e. A righteous lifestyle. Black people have never had the opportunity to serve or worship their own God and practice their own way of life, until now! White people or the Devil denied black people (So Called Negroes) this basic human right. There are many whites in America that feel that they do not owe the black man anything because he has being paid. That is the same as Delilah (America) telling Sampson (SO-Called Negroes) that it is alright that I blinded you because I am going to give you a job (Pay You so much a week), and you should be satisfied. This Delilah (America) acts like she does not realize that Sampson wants his eye-sight returned, return to his own people, eat his own food, and return to praying to his own God. These are the spiritual assets taken from the Blackman in America that have not been returned. Therefore, White People, Gog and Magog have not paid their debt to black people (Just as in Sampson's days, sometime, the whole house must come down) one thing is for certain, God is in the plan.

Cain and Abel

Another name used in the Bible to identify White people is Cain. The name Cain represents white people and Abel represents black people; the Bible uses symbolic names like Cain and Abel to indicate a situation or characteristisc between the two people, and now to the story. Geneis 4: 1–2, And Adam knew Eve his wife; and she conceived, and bare Cain, and said, I have gotten a man from the Lord. And she again bare his brother Abel, and Abel was a keeper of sheep, but Cain was a tiller of the ground.

And it came to pass that Cain brought an offering to the Lord, and Abel also made an offering to the Lord. The Lord had respect for the offering of Abel, but he did not have respect for Cain's offering. God explained to Cain that if he does well, then his offering would be accepted, however, if he does not well, it is because "Sin" lieth at the door. Cain was angry, (because he had to prove himself righteous), and while in the field, Cain slew his brother Abel. And the Lord said unto Cain, Where is thy brother Abel, his blood crieth to me from the ground. Cain said, I do not know, Am I my brother's keeper?

God cursed Cain and said that henceforth he shall be a vagabond and fugitive throughout the earth. Cain said that if this comes to pass then everyone that find me will slay me, but God put a "mark" on Cain so that no one would kill him when they found him. The "mark on Cain" (White People) was that his *identity* was concealed from the rest of the human family so that none actually knew who he was (A born killer or the Devil) and he could live out his days of 6,000 years. Cain would be safe to live on the earth as long as God had his "Mark" on him, but once God removed his mark or revealed his identity, his time would be up (God revealed his identity July 4, 1930). Cain left the presence of the Lord, and dwelt in the land of Nod, on the East of Eden, i.e. Europe. Cain represents a nation of people or the Europeans, and the biblical account of Cain slew Abel is the European Nations killing the Black People throughout the world; they have killed six-hundred million or one hundred million blacks for every thousand years on the earth!

CHAPTER VIII
Behold, I Send You Elijah (To establish A New Moral-System and Economy for the Blackman)

Islam Will Set the Negroes free by Restoring Their Identity

These two scriptures are the basis for the Hon. Elijah Muhammad coming into the world as the Messenger of Allah. Holy Quran 35:24 Surely we have sent thee with the Truth as a bearer of good news and a warner. And there is not a people but a warner has gone among them. Bible Malachi 4: 5–6 verses Behold, I will send you Elijah, the prophet, before the coming of the great and dreadful day of the Lord; 6 And he shall turn the hearts of the fathers to the children, and the hearts of the children to their fathers, lest I come and smite the earth with a curse.

Elijah Muhammad was born Elijah Poole, October 7, 1897, in Sandersville, Ga. United States of America, A So Called Negro, that had been lost in this Cave known as America for 375 years from his own native people. America is known scripturally as a Cave for the Negroes because they were shut off from the rest of the world culturally, educationally, economically, religiously, and eventually became blind, deaf, and dumb to civilized life. One day, he heard a voice, saying La ilaha illa Allah, (There is no God but Allah) this voice was none other than Master Fard Muhammad (God in Person).

Elijah kept coming to the temple until Master Fard Muhammad revealed to him that he was the Elijah of Malachi 4:5–6 of the Bible, and the Prophet Muhammad of the Holy Quran. The So-Called Negroes were scripturally described as Arabs, and that our people had been hidden in Scripture as well as in reality. All of this was done so that the devil could live out his time until God comes and set up a new nation to rule forever. He told Elijah that he was to preach THE TRUTH called Islam. Which means entire submission to the Will of God. The essence of Islam is peace, and the one that submits to Islam and bears witness that Allah is God and Muhammad is his Messenger is a Muslim. Other Prophets of Islam are Abraham, Moses, Jesus and Muhammad of 1400 years ago. Scripturally, Moses received the Torah, Jesus received the Gospel and Muhammad received the Holy Quran; Elijah Muhammad received the Truth of them all Torah, Gospel and Holy Quran).

The statement from the Holy Quran 35:24 And there is not a people but a warner has gone among them; shows conclusively that the Hon. Elijah Muhammad was a Divine messenger because no one ever came among the So-Called Negroes with a Divine Message. Just as Allah revealed himself to Prophet Muhammad of fourteen hundred years ago in a Cave known as Mount Hira in Arabia, and told him that he was the Messenger of Allah and his mission was to build a nation of muslims; So it is today, that Allah in the person of Master Fard Muhammad commissioned Elijah Poole, later (Muhammad) to be his messenger and build a nation of muslims out of the So-Called Negroes. Elijah also received his calling to be the Messenger of Allah in a Cave known as the United States of America. (A cave for the Negroes because it shuts out all light of understanding and progress for the blackman). The negroes have never had a Divine warner or Messenger before Elijah Muhammad.

Prophet Muhammad of fourteen hundred years ago real mission was to unite the fractured and scattered tribes of Arabs into a united nation bearing witness that there is only one God and his proper name is Allah. His mission lasted twenty-three years, and the revelation that was revealed to him during this time was compiled into a book called the Holy Quran. This is the Muslim Bible. In this book, Allah revealed who was the troublemaker on earth in Chapter 18, titled the Cave. The holy Quran revealed the history of the Children of Israel (White People) and how they had gone around the world preaching lies that Jesus was God in order to rule the people with falsehood. Muhammad started a Holy War against the infidels known as the crusades.

Muhammad's war against them was not totally successful because he (like Jesus before him) read in scripture that he was too soon and that the Devil (White people) had thirteen hundred more years to rule the earth with tricks and lies. So he stopped the war, but the devils were set back one thousand years in their progress. This revelation broke Muhammad's heart and he died at the age of sixty-three.

Now Elijah Muhammad's mission was similar to Mohamet, only he comes at the end of the Devil's time to rule over the earth (six-thousand years) Revelation 13:18 Here is wisdom. Let him that hath understanding count the number of the beast; for it is the number of a man; and his number is six hundred, three score and six. It took six hundred years to make the Devil on the Isle of Patmos Rev 1:9, and three score is sixty times one hundred years equal six thousand years of rulership, and six equals the six days of the week which spiritually means that he (Devil would rule for six days and the seventh day he would rest), a day with God is as a thousand years. The seventh day of rest is when the blackman would regain his power over the earth.

Furthermore, the nation that Prophet Mohamet started would be completed in Messenger Elijah Muhammad. The Arab nations are just as divided today as they were when Prophet Mohamet came to them fourteen hundred years ago; and they all have the Holy Quran but they are still divided. Messenger Muhammad's job is to raise a completely dead people to life, mentally, spiritually, economically, establish a home with some land, create an identity, and establish the fact that God is not just a spirit but manifest as a human being. Once all of this is done, then the Arabs and the world will know that Allah is God (Master Fard Muhammad) and that Elijah Muhammad is his Messenger, and that the So-Called Negroes is his chosen people to lead the nations of earth.

Now that the identity of the Hon. Elijah Muhammad is established as the Messenger of Allah, let us look at his mission. He was taught for three and one half years by Master Fard Muhammad concerning every phase of life. His guide (other than God) is the Holy Quran) his mental pattern is to establish a New Muslim Nation. New in some concepts but the Beliefs remain the same. He must restore the negroes identity. He must establish new dietary habits because they are accustomed to eating poison (pig). New dress codes because the devil has undressed the people and showed the world their shame. A new muslim nation must be established!

When the Supreme Being (Fard Muhammad) came to America, he said that the So-Called Negroes live in a cage that is 3,615,211 square miles, which is the circumference of the United States, and that the negro is walking backwards and forward in this cage like a lion. He has been doing this for over four hundred years looking for the "door to his salvation." The door that would tell him, who he is? What time is spiritually? What should he be doing at this time? Well finally the door has arrived in the person of the Supreme Being himself (Master Fard Muhammad). He has brought Islam as the door (Way of Life) to answer all our questions and fulfill all our needs. The Nation of Islam under the leadership of his messenger, Elijah Muhammad, will set the negroes in heaven, at once.

The government, Nation of Islam, is designed to give the negroes back their original names, culture, history, flag, and teach them the values of Freedom, Justice, and Equality as other nations of earth. But first, the negroes must realize that they have been poisoned in mind and spirit by the devil. They must be re-orientated to their own way of life called Islam. This re-orientation process is known as the Resurrection of the Dead 1 Corinthians 15th Chapter. New rules of living must be established. They must be cleaned up and made fit to rule themselves and then to rule others in righteousness because the devil has poisoned the whole world with his filthy way of life. Negroes Minds are like "frozen embryos."

The Bible teaches that Jesus came to save the Jews and build a new government, but he failed in his mission, and the world is looking for his return to complete the job. The Jesus of two-thousand years ago is dead and will not return because physically dead people do not return to this earth. Now, spirirually dead people is another matter. Fard Muhammad is that modern-day Jesus that the world is looking for and the Kingdom that he will establish is with the So-Called Negroes and not the Jews. They have had all the kingdoms they are going to get! The Supreme Being is the one that will raise the dead "Spiritually and Mentally" not Physically. No Physically Dead People can come back to life!

These are some of the restricted laws of Islam that when practiced by the Negroes will resurrect back to life "spiritually and mentally" to the reality of God. Exodus 19:25 Moses brings the Law to the people.

"Restricted Laws of Islam"

All Believers must strickly obey these laws; mere Belief counts for nothing unless carried into practice.

1. Obey Allah, his Apostle and believe in the message sent to you as told by the messenger.
2. Obedience to his Apostle is obedience to Allah, as the messenger is the bearer of Allah's message. Respect to the messenger is respect to Allah.
3. Worship no God but Allah, the one that the messenger represents to you.
4. Fear no one but Allah.
5. Obey those in authority among you, and obey non-believers in authority over you as long as it does not conflict with your religion.
6. No drinking (Wine, Whiskey, beer, ale, alcohol or other intoxicant).
7. It is forbidden to commit fornication or adultery.
8. It is forbidden to eat the pig or its by-products.
9. No insubordination, slack talk or gossip.
10. Do not lust.
11. Do not associate with those in bad standing.
12. No gambling of any kind (Numbers, dice cards, games of chance).
13. No smoking of any kind (Reefers or cigarettes, cigar or pipe).
14. No Dope (Herion, cocaine, or any kind of dope or drugs).
15. No lying (Speak the truth regardless of circumstances).
16. No Stealing.
17. Do not deal with hypocrites or show sympathy with them (Individuals that were in the Nation and now works against the Nation).
18. Do not commit acts of violence on ourselves or others.
19. Do unto other as you would want others to do unto you.
20. Must be clean at all times (Mind and Body).
21. Spend of what Allah has given you in the cause of Islam.
22. Love brother and sister believer as yourself.

23. Be kind and do good to all.
24. Kill no one whom Allah has not ordered to be killed.

These laws were specifically designed for the So-Called Negroes to clean up their morals, and raise them spiritually and mentally to be a civilized nation of people. These Beliefs in Islam have not changed since the days of Moses or Mohamet of fourteen hundred years ago.

Beliefs In Islam

1. Belief in one God, whose proper name is Allah.
2. Belief in all the Prophets, and the Scriptures they brought to the world.
3. Belief in Charity.
4. Belief in Prayer and Fasting.
5. Belief in the Hajj (The Muslim Pilgrimage to Mecca once in your lifetime.

Malachi 4:5

Behold, I send you Elijah, the prophet, before the evening of the great and dreadful day of the Lord; And he shall turn the heart of the fathers to the children, and the heart of the children to their fathers, lest I come and smite the earth with a curse. He will turn the hearts of the father to the children by using the Muslim Program given to him by God (Master Fard Muhammad) as stated above.

Orthodox Jews

When the So-Called Negroes (blacks) have been cleaned up and living a civilized life like other nations of earth, then what people will they resemble spiritually? Naturally, they will still be black people but their life-style will resemble the Orthodox Jews. The Orthodox Jews are similar to the blacks of America in many ways.

A. The Jews have had a holocaust in Germany. i.e. The Blacks have had a holocaust in America.

B. The Jews do not ever want to forget, lest the same condition repeat itself. i.e. The Blacks to not ever want to forget lest the same is repeated.

C. The Jews were killed and held prisoners in Nazi concentration camps i.e. The Blacks were killed and held slaves on plantations.

D. The whiteman was the enemy to both Jews and Blacks.

E. The Jews have their own God, culture, history, religion, and Way of Life; Dietary Laws and Private Schools.

The Muslims (Blacks) have their own God culture, history, religion, and Way of Life; Dietary Laws and Private Schools.

The new nation that Hon. Elijah Muhammad was to build out of the So-Called Negroes is the Nation of Islam. However, all nations have some similarity to others and the people most similar to the Muslims in the Nation of Islam is the Orthodox Jews. The average white person worries that the Nation of Islam is based on revenge for wrongs done to the black man, but that is not the case. God will fight the battle of past injustices and not the nation In fact, the believers in Allah, under the direction of the Hon. Elijah Muhammad are not allowed to carry weapons of any kind. So the focus is on building a nation, and not tearing down a people! But, the history of the whiteman will be taught until our people are raised up and on their own as a nation, with their own Money-System.

A lot of ill feeling could be erased between black and white if this country (U.S.A.) paid the Reparation that was due the blackman for all of those years of forced labor (310 years). The African countries are asking reparation for the ones that were taken from their land by force once the identities can be ascertained. This problem must be solved so that that the blackman can be put back on his feet like the Japanese and Germans after World War II. (They were paid reparation; Why not the Blackman of America?) This problem will be solve by God, it is call the Law of Requital! It means that every action has its reaction; if an action is good then there is a reward coming. However, if the action is evil, then there is a consequence for that action. What America has done is evil to the blackman and if not addressed and solved, then the consequences must come according to the Law.

Nichodemus and Jesus

This section is concerning the new birth of the So-Called Negroes, and Nicodemus and Jesus gives some insight into being born again. John 3: 1–14 There was a man named Nicodemus, a ruler of the Jews 4. Nichodemus said unto him, How can a man be born when he is old? Can he enter the second time into his mother's womb, and be born? 5 Jesus answered, Verily, Verily, I say unto thee, Except a man be born of water and of the Spirit, He cannot enter the Kingdom of God. 6 That which is born of flesh is flesh and that which is born of Spirit is Spirit. 14 And as Moses lifted up the serpent in the wilderness, even so must the Son of Man be lifted up, 15 that whosoever believeth in him should not perish, but have eternal life.

The Negroes will be "Born Again" and receive eternal life by believing in this truth taught by the Son of Man (Master Fard Muhammad), just as the serpent (white people) were lifted up in the wilderness (Europe) and put on their feet by believing in their teacher, Moses. Just as Moses spiritually gave birth "Born Again" to white people in the caves and hillsides of Europe and they went forth and built a world for themselves; so it is that the wisdom of God (master Fard Muhammad) will give spiritual birth to the minds of the Negroes in this Cave called America.

With this knowledge, they will build a new muslim nation of their own!

Separation is the key to building this new muslim nation! Not physical separation but mental and spiritual separation! The negroes must be "Born Again" in their own religion, culture, history, and their own concept of God. Spiritually they were born into the Whiteman's Religion, history, his culture, as their own because they (negroes) had no alternative. But All praise are due to Allah in the person of Master Fard Muhammad, there is now an alternative way of life, Islam. If black people do not accept their own way of life then they will not be accepted by God in the new Kingdom, because their ways and habits have been corrupted by the Devil, and Allah will not accept them. They must be a righteous, clean people morally and spiritually to be the People of God.

The Stone That The Builders Rejected

Matthew Ch. 21 42–44 Jesus said unto them, Did ye never read in the scriptures, The stone which the builders rejected, the same is become the head of the corner; this is the Lord's doing, and it is marvelous in our eyes?

43 Therefore say I unto you, The Kingdom of God shall be taken from you, and given to a nation bringing forth the fruits of it.

44 And whosoever shall fall on this stone shall be broken, but on whom soever it shall fall, it will grind him to powder.

The stone in this parable of Jesus is the So-Called Negroes whom (God) Master Fard Muhammad will make into a great nation with power, under his guidance, known as the Kingdom of God. Anyone trying to destroy this work is playing with fire, and will be ground into powder. The stone that has been rejected by the whole world as a nation is the So-Called Negroes of America. and the builders (leading nations) will be brought low, as Allah build spiritually into the negroes a foundation of righteousness above the other nations of earth. This is known scripturally as Raising a Dead Nation To Life, Holy Quran, Ch. 6, Section 15, Verse 817 states that not only were the dead raised to life, but they had now with them the light by which they showed the way to others.

Although despised and rejected (negroes) by the world-community as nothing, God as chosen the negroes as his People. God's light is the brightest light of all in this world of darkness, but since his light is reflected by people who practice his ways and behavior, it takes a little time to manifest into full bloom among the negroes but it is growing. The light that God brings to the negroes is Islam, and the book is the Holy Quran, and the interpretation is from Allah himself, and not from the scholars of the devil's world. No nation has been more spiritually blind, deaf, and dumb than the negroes, when they wake up (and they will) it will fulfill the scriptures in Genesis 15:13 that after four hundred years, God will come and bring them out with great substance after being afflicted and rejected by the builders of the world.

The Stone (So Called Negroes) that the builders (Communities of the world) rejected will become the head of the corner (World Community). Matthew 43 and 4 Jesus said therefore say I unto you, The Kingdom of God shall be taken from you (European Nations), and given to a nation bringing forth the fruits of it. And whosoever shall fall on this stone shall be broken, but on whomsoever it shall fall, it will ground him to powder. The Kingdom of God has been given to the European Nations of the world for 6,000 years, the fish, fowl, land, sea, sky, other nations, and everything on the earth. The Kingdom of God is simply the earth and all that dwells within it or above it! The Europeans have been unable to bring forth the fruits of Salvation (Righeous Living according to the Divine Law) to the population of the earth. In fact, they have destroyed most of the earth since they have been the overseer! Now, God has decided to take the Kingdom from them and give it to another people that will be taught how to rule the Kingdom of God with Righteousness and Justice.

The people selected by God (Master Fard Muhammad) to rule the next government of Righteousness is none other than the So-Called Negroes of America. If this seems impossible to you, it is because you are judging the Blackman and Woman of America by their current state of Mind and living conditions. It was the same in Pharaoh's days when he laughed at the very thought of his slaves having a Government of their own and ruling themselves. Because he knew that he had not taught them how to govern self, or they had no economy, no land, no connections with other governments, and most of all the slaves loved Pharaoh (white people). So, in reality, it looks like a case in futility trying to raise the Negroes to a level of self-sufficiency, but all things are possible with God. Allah has said that the Negroes will become the cornerstone of the world, then it will be. The method that he is using to teach the Negroes is called Divine Guidance! He is the one building this Nation of Righteousness; He is using the Negroes to prove his Power and to show that he is in the world today bringing about a universal change.

Why is the So-Called Negroes of America so hated and despised all over the world? Why are they homeless within the whiteman's culture? Why do other blackmen and women still have a homeland and culture to call their own? What was the Negroes original Language? Why is the Blackman and Woman referred to as Negroes and other blacks on earth referred to as Jamaican, Nigerian, Haitian or Ethiopian. It is because all other black nations on earth still have their nationality, language, and culture, and the poor Blackman of America has been robbed of his Nationality, Flag, Religion, and Culture here in America through slavery. The worst part of this tragedy is that the whiteman has no intention of returning these vital elements of a nation through Reparation for re-building, Education via Afrocentricity, Islam as their Religion, or even the acknowledgement that they named the Blackman a Negro as a symbol that he was Dead mentally to his own way of life. Mentally, from Black to White.

As a result of the mental and spiritual condition (Dead to the knowledge of Self) of the Negroes of America, this has caused them to be despised and rejected not only by the whiteman, but other black nations of earth because they feel superior to the blackman of America because they still have their Culture and Nationality. However, what the other Black Nations fail to realize is that the So-Called Negroes is their long lost brother (Joseph) that was sold into slavery as a testimony to the Glory of God and will one day be the instrument to resurrect them from their mental and spiritual death. This is taken place today because God has chosen the Negroes to rebuild the world Genesis 15:13 Know of a surety that thy seed shall be a sojourner in a land that is not their, and shall serve them; and they shall afflict them four hundred years. The time is up (1555–1955), and now the History, Culture, and Religion is being taught; Our Flag is the Sun, Moon and Stars (Crescent), Our Nation, Philsophy, and Way of Life is Islam. The land, Economy, is on its way, Believe it or Not! The Blackman and Woman of America are not Negroes but a people fulfilling Scripture and Prophecy; they are Divine People! It is God that uplifts the downtrodden.

Some definitions of a stone are as follows; Material used for construction. A gem or precious stone. A piece of rock finished for a particular purpose. Why did Jesus use the word Stone to refer to a rejected people that would one day become the corner-stone of the new world. He used the word "Stone" to refer to the So-Called Negroes because they are a people that are precious in the eyesight of God, and must be re-constructed mentally and spiritually, and made fit for a particular purpose in God's plan for a new government. The finished product would be a people so strong in the Ways and Habits of God that they would be the Corner-stone of Righteousness for other nations of earth to emulate and pattern them selves after. First, an example of how the Blackman of America has been torn down in reference to his identity.

After being brought to America and made slaves physically, the slave-master started re-naming the Blackman by calling him a Nigger, Colored, Negro, and now Afro-American. The root of this identity-crisis is to keep the blackman from knowing his real identity. Nigger is an offensive term meaning stingy or miserly, and cannot be a peoples identity. Negro means dead or insensitive to one's self, a tool, unaware. The word was adopted in Latin meaning the people living along the Niger River (Niger-Nigger-Negro-Black) in Africa and used the term to symbolize all black people, which in reality has nothing to do with their identity. But since the whiteman was given power to write the dictionaries and encylopedias he wrote history in such a way as to indicate that the Blackman has no identity other than the Niger Riger or his skin color.

Now, to being colored. The So-Called Negroes cannot be colored because the Blackman is the Father of all colors or races, and the originator cannot equal of that which he makes. For example. Black is the original Color, i.e. From Black comes colors or that which is color-ed. Color-ed means past tensed that which came from the original color. The colors that comes from Black are Brown (Japanese Race), Red (Indians), Yellow (chinese) and the White (Caucausian Race). These races are Color-ed, Brown, Yellow, Red, and White, and should be referred to as the Colored People of the earth.

Now that we know the Blackman is not the Colored Man; let us understand this term Afro-American. This term Afro-American is an attemp to link the blackman of

America to his heritage, and it is a complimentary term in its concept. However, it indicates an extension of the Blackman through time and does not include the re-making of the blackman's mind here in America, God came to America and gave the Negroes their "Spiritual Identity" which has within it the History, Culture, Religion, Flag, Origin and Identity. The Blackman's Spiritual Identity is a Muslim, which means entire submission to the Will of God. A muslim is the very nature of the blackman and was the system in which he created himself in the beginning of time. I am not talking about Fourteen hundred years ago with some Arab or Prophet Muhammed.

I am talking about the Blackman! Muslim is a modern day-term that indicates a state of mind. A Mind of Righteousness. This is the Mind or type of Mentality needed to build the Kingdom of God. A spiritual identity is first because unless the moral fiber of the negroes is changed; there will be no kingdom. All nations of earth have a religion in which they get their identity. In order to be modern, the blackman must have a modern religion. Christians have Christianity (Whites), Jews have Judaism (Whites), Japanese and Chinese have Buddaism, and the Blackman has Islam. Islam as taught by the Hon. Elijah Muhammad takes us beyond Prophet Muhammad, into the very nature and creation of Civilization. The reason for this is because God is guiding this nation with Divine Revelation of who the Blackman is and every other nation on this earth.

Remember, Islam is the psychological term that embodies the knowledge that God is using to raise the blackman and woman up to a civilized state of mind. Remember, this is a new nation being raised, not the old orthodox Islam of the past, but new concepts of Man, new ideas on how to eat, new understandings about heaven and hell, new perspective on re-incarnation, new understanding of God and the Devil, and most of all, the opportunity to build a new government based on Peace, Justice, and Equality for all Men.

One of the many falsehoods that God intends to change for the So-Called Negroes is his dietary laws (habits of eating). This scripture is taken from the Holy Quran 5:3 in which Allah instructs the Negroes on what to eat.

Forbidden to you is that which dies of itself, and blood, and flesh of swine, and that on which any other name than that of Allah has been invoked, and the strangled (animal), and that of beaten to death, and that killed by a fall, and that killed by goring with a horn, and that which wild beast have eaten—except what you slaughter, and that which is sacrificed on stones set up (for idols), and that you seek to divide by arrows; that is a transgression. This day have those who disbelieve despaired of your religion, so fear them not, and fear me. This day have I perfected for you your religion and completed my favor to you and chosen for you Islam as a religion.

Notice carefully that Allah (God) says that he chose Islam for the Negroes "*As a Religion*" "*As A Religion,*" because in truth, Islam is our nature meaning to submit to God. It is given to the Blackman "As a Religion" in order for him to have a methodology or path-way back to himself, or back to God. In reality, Islam is not a religion at all, it is the natural Way of Life for the Blackman, However, today's world is so controlled by Religion that Allah chose Islam as the best religion for the blackman under the circumstances. Once the Kingdom of God is re-established, then the Blackman will once again be living according to natural laws and righteousness. These different religions were established by Prophets, and with God ruling his own Kingdom, there will be no need for all these different religion, (only one); Entire submission to the Will of God and his Laws.

But at the present time, God forbids the Negroes to eat Swine (Pig). The swine is a grafted animal between the Cat, Rat, and the Dog. He has the dog's body, the cat's ears, and the rat's tail. He has 999 germs in his body and a sewage line between his split hoof, that runs pus and if plugged up it would kill him instantly. He is so poisonous that he can take poison, (eat snakes) and it will not harm him. He is ugly, greedy, and is shyless and careless. Once a person begins to eat this creature, they lose shyness, and a portion of their natural beauty appearance.

CHAPTER IX
The Real History of Pharaoh (White People) and Children of Israel

Blackman's Identity Was Stolen From Him

The theme or purpose of this book is to give scriptural evidence that the Blackman of America has been robbed of his Identity as the people of God, and the time has now come in history wherein that stolen identity is being restored back to him. The So Called Negro is another name used to deceive the blackman as to his real identity (God's People). Children of Israel, Lazarus, Lost Sheep and Joseph are other names used to describe the Blackman of America and his condition before being brought into slavery, while in slavery, and after he comes out of slavery (mental and economical) with the help of God and his Messenger (Elijah Muhammad). Restoring the Blackman's identity back to him, which is,"the Seed of Abraham" that was lost in a land (America) that is not theirs for over 400 years, is the last step in the Resurrection of the Dead, and then the Judgement of the world will set in. But first, the Blackman must Wake-Up to who he is, then the Judgement!

Today, in America, the So Called Negroes minds are enslaved by the false teachings of the Devil (white people) as to life, and how the two people came together. In order to understand how the Blackman came to America, I will use the story of Joseph written in the Bible, Genesis Chapter 37 wherein the Blackman (Joseph) is sold into slavery and given a new name, Chapter 41; and now, let us proceed into our story!

When Joseph was a lad of seventeen, he had a dream and he told it to his brothers. Genesis 37:7 For behold, we were binding sheaves in the field, and lo, my sheaf arose, and also stood upright; and, behold, your sheaves stood around about, and made obeisance to my sheaf. Joseph (So Called Negroes) are hated and rejected by his brothers for this prophecy, and they said, shall thou have dominion over us? And he dreamed another dream and told it to his brethren, and said Behold I have dreamed a dream more; and behold, the sun, and the moon, and the eleven stars made obeisance to me.

Joseph father's name was Jacob (His father's spititual name was Israel) and his father made Joseph a coat of many colors, which symbolized the many different people of the earth. Joseph brothers plotted his death because of his dreams and it came to pass that one day, Joseph was with his brothers and they stripped Joseph of his coat, and cast him into a pit. They lifted up their eyes and said, look a company of Ishmaelites, going to Egypt (America). Why kill him? Let us sell him, and Joseph (So Called Negroes) were sold into slavery and brought to America. Many were kidnapped. Their clothes were smeared with blood (like Joseph coat of many colors) and many fathers and mothers never saw their children again, and they mourned their loss. Remember, Joseph's father (Original Black People) spiritual name is Israel, therefore the So-Called Negroes real identity is the Children of Israel).

Joseph (Black Man) was brought to America, and made a slave. The first Black People that landed in America could not speak English, because their native tongue was Arabic. Their God was Allah, and their Religion was Islam. They were from Egypt, and their civilization was along the Nile River and the Euphrates. Their Culture was refined and exihits are displayed in museums throughout the world. They (So Called Negroes) are descendants of the first people of the earth, and the creators of all the races and sciences of modern societies such as: Law, Astronomy, Chemistry, Agriculture and Mathematics. The first blacks to land in America never heard the word Negro, they were made Negroes when they arrived in America, and now to explain how it happened. From Black to Negro.

Biblically, let us not forget Joseph's dreams or prophecy of one day being the ruler over his brothers, and the Sun, Moon, and Stars making obeisance to him; Joseph was from the land of Canaan, Canaan gets its name from Noah's son Ham (who was black). Joseph and his brothers were Canaanites and today we call them Africans because of their blood relationship to other nations on the African continent, instead of Hamites or Canaanites.

The Making of a Negro's Mind; A Mind of Dependency!

Joseph (Blacks) first landed in America as slaves in 1555, they did not come out of the jungles of Africa, but from Egypt, down on the River Nile. They were not savages (uncivilized) when they came to America but were made uncivilized (savages) when they got here. The white people (scripturally known as the Devil or Satan) allowed the original black people to have babies, and they took the babies and instilled fear in them to obey everything they said. They told the children that they were from monkies and were swinging on trees when the whites found them. They (whites) refused to allow them to know their background, culture, religion, God, or anything of their past, and also refuse to allow any asiactic influence to come near the slaves (Joseph).

They worked the blacks from sunup to sundown constantly instilling fear as to who was the master. They allowed no education to penetrate their minds until all they knew was "Yes Master and No Master". They (blacks) were reduced to one-third human being and two-thirds of a burden bearing beast (Mule). After sixty-four years of this treatment and the devils (white people) were positive that no light (knowledge) was in his mind about who he was—then they named Joseph (blacks) a Negro. Which means a black person that is not self-guided but rather is guided by white people, and is dead to the knowledge of who he really is. This is the true meaning of Negro. No other people on earth are called So-Called Negroes except the Blackman of America, who under went this form of enslavement wherein their identity was stolen and replaced by a false identity. A Negro's Mind is like a "frozen embryo" waiting to thaw out!

After stealing the blackman's identity (Joseph) then Pharaoh (white people) gave the slaves their names Genesis 41:45. The slaves were given the white man Names, Religion, his concept of God or Jesus Christ, his interpretation that God was in the sky and the devil in ground.

Many black people are still using white peoples name today, still practicing the white man's religion, and still believing that the Devil is in the ground and God is in the sky looking down on them. What a Shame! Later on. the explanation will be given as to why the devil did this to black people as revenge for what was done to him four-thousand years ago in the caves and hills of Europe. But for now, let us leave this point with the fact that Joseph is in slavery, he has been made a Negro (Dead to the knowledge of who he is), he has been given a new name (Names of White People) and he is roaming around America thinking that he is free. Poor Slave! The time is 1857 and the Blackman has been a slave in America for a little over Two-Hundred years. Genesis 15:13 says that they would be slaves for four-hundred years. THE BLACKMAN'S MENTAL AND SPIRITUAL IDENTITY WAS STOLEN IN SLAVERY; AND REPLACED WITH A NEW SLAVERY IDENTITY CALLED A NEGRO. "THIS NEW MENTALITY SPIRITUALLY KILLED HIS KNOWLEDGE OF SELF."

Dred Scott Decision

On July 4, 1776, when the United States of America was founded as an independent Government, the slaves (Joseph) was not included in the Constitution and therefore was not considered a citizen of this country but rather as property of white people. The slaves (blacks) were counted as property (cattle, houses or sheeps) owned by white slave-masters! This is important to remember (they were not citizens but property). Which brings us to the Dred Scott Decision.

Dr. John Emerson (white man) was a surgeon in the army from St Louis, Missouri and he was assigned to duty at Rock Island, Illinois. Accompanying him on these travels was his slave, Dred Scott. In 1838, he returned to Missouri and later, Dr. Emerson died. After his death, Dred Scott, along with the help of a friendly lawyer brought suit in the Missouri courts for his liberty, arguing that his residence in Illinois where slavery was barred under the Northwest Ordinance and the Missouri Compromise had made him a free man. On March 6, 1857, the high court declared "That Negroes were not Citizens; therefore Dred Scott could not sue in a federal court."

Negroes Minds Were "Made" During Slavery

Dred Scott did nor realize that as long as he remain a Negro in America that he would always be the property of White People; because the Mind of White People was instilled into the Negroes by a process called Grafting. In real reality, Grafting is the unionizing of one product with a dis-similar product and the outcome is A THIRD PRODUCT that is different from the first two products. The third product in this case is the Negro Mentality created in the Black Man. Here are some examples of grafting by the white man.

Take fruit for instance, the white man takes two natural fruits (lemon and the orange) and combines them and makes a grapefruit. The grapefruit is not a natural fruit (made by God) but rather a grafted fruit made by the devil. In the animal world, he took the (horse and donkey) and made a mule. The mule is sterile and can't reproduce himself. The mule is symbolic of the negro because the negro can't think for himself because he does not have his own culture, religion, or way of life in order to think from. Next, let us look at the Hog, which is another grafted animal. The hog was made by combining the (Cat, Rat and Dog), look closely and you will see the rat's tail, the cat's ears, and the dog's body. He is filthy and was made to eat filth therefore he is forbidden by God to be eaten for human consumption.

    The white man entire world is grafted; made from combining other human, animals, fruits, plants, or any elements in order to produce a world for himself. Why grafting? Because the white man himself is a grafted being by combining different races over a period of time (600 years) until the Caucasian Race was made. The process is call Human Birth Control, and it is practice all over the earth. This is the method used to produce the Negroes Mind. The white man put his thinking into the Blackman and refused to allow him to think any other way for 310 years (He blocked out all other avenues of thinking), He totally remade (grafted) his Mind and Spirit to worship him. He birthed the Negro into existence with Name, Dietary laws, religion and a government by Mental Birth Control.

CHAPTER X
Blacks Are Slaves By Law and Economics!

1868 The Fourteenth Amendment

One of the biggest tricks of all was to make the Negro think that he has finally arrived because he is now a "citizen" of the United States. After the Civil War, many issues had to be decided about the Negroes, and his freedom. Neither President Lincoln nor his running-mate Andrew Johnson were trying to free the slaves but rather unite the nation. After Lincoln was assassinated, then President Johnson took office and his statement about the negroes was "Damn the negroes, I am fighting their masters, these treacherous Aristocrats. I wish to God, every head of a family in the United States had one slave (black) to take the drudgery and menial work off his family." He signed into law the Thirteenth Amendment abolishing slavery. Remember, Negroes have been Dead to their own way of life (Islam).

In 1865, Congress passed a Civil Rights Act (Which President Johnson vetoed, saying it was unconstitutional) which, besides declaring that Negroes were citizens of the United States, denied the states the power to restrict their rights to testify in court and to hold property. However, this was a little too late for Dred Scott. In June 1866, Congress passed and submitted to the states, a new amendment to the Constitution, the fourteenth amendment. This amendment gave a broad definition of American Citizenship: All persons born or naturalized in the United States, and subject to the jurisdiction thereof, are citizens of the United States and of the State wherein they reside. No State shall make or enforce any laws that deprive the privileges or immunities of any citizens, nor deprive any citizen of life, liberty, or property. Now, here is the trick to this concocted citizenship.

The negroes still could not vote. Segregation was in full force. Negroes were not given back their Names, Nationality, Culture, or Identity. They were still in Mental and Economic Slavery!! They were still lynched, beaten, and killed whenever the whiteman felt the urge. The devil had children by the black woman whenever he pleased. What government perform these acts on its citizens. NEGROES ARE NOT CITIZENS OF THE UNITED STATES.

1955 Desegregation of the Schools

The time is now approaching 400 years of being in a strange land with strangers (genesis 15:13 1555–1955) and being afflicted. At this point in time, the slaves (Joseph) is totally blind, deaf, and dumb to the knowledge of himself and the outside world of his kind. The slave has been segregated ever since being in America, and now that the time has arrived "ECONOMICALLY" for him to go free,"mentally", the white man tries his most effective trick to keep the Blackman enslaved, and it is called Integration.

A trick is a deceptive strategy used to deceive a people. White people realized that their worse nightmare was for the Negroes to be separate and free in America; A nation within nation. Also, they realize that the negroes greatest desire was to become a member of the white world, because he was blind, deaf, and dumb to himself. So, they came up with a new strategy of control called Integration. This method would allow the master to control every aspect of the slave (Blacks) existence. This method would be based on "mental and spiritual control", just as the ball and chain was for physical control. Integration is a mental and Economical trick that keep blacks from seeing Whites for who they really are—the oppressors of Black People.

After 1955, the time given by God for enslavement, the slave (blacks) are free to do as they please (physically, Mentally, and Spiritually) but they are unable to "Do For Self" because they accepted this trick of Integration and have not built a foundation or base for themselves. However, God is in the plan, and a base or foundation is being prepared for the negroes. But, let us review a case and see how Integration works in the 1955 Desegration of the Schools.

Don't forget that up until this point in history, the negroes have been totally segregated from white people, murdered, castrated, history destroyed, and given new identities in the devil's society as slaves, and now they want to integrate WITH THEIR SLAVES! DON'T BELIEVE IT! A man or people that will not "treat you right," will not "teach" you right. The 1954 Brown v. Board of Education of Topeka case which challenged the "Separate but Equal Doctrine in Education was declared unconstitutional and the Supreme Court ordered the States to proceed with all deliberate speed to "integrate the schools."

Of course, the slaves were happy and felt that they had won a major victory. But look at the results, white people controlled the curriculum and they were given a history called Negro History. This history further poisoned their minds and caused them to hate themselves. It portrayed the blacks as "monkeys swinging on trees" when they were rescued by whites and brought to America. (AN OUTRIGHT LIE). The whiteman was the one swinging on trees during the days when he was a caveman living in the caves and hillsides of Europe. In fact, the reason that the whiteman brought the blackman into slavery and keeps him in this condition was for casting him out of heaven (Middle East) and into the wilderness for breaking the laws of God, Read Genesis 22:24. This entire episode of the Blackman and Whiteman in America is an act of REVENGE on the part of the whiteman. But (Devil) made a great mistake because no-one can kill and disgrace God's people (Joseph) and get away it. Gal. 6:7 Be not deceived, God is not mocked, for whatever a man soweth, that shall he also reap.

Education is a tool for molding and shaping the mind. First, they (white people) shaped the blackman a history (Negro History), then they established the organizations that they would recognize as representatives for negroes, such as, NAACP, Urban League or some Church Group SCLC. The Negro leadership was usually a preacher of Christianity (Devils' Religion). Christianity shapes the Negroes "spiritual mind" to accept white people as God's people. The only thing that has been truly integrated is the Minds of black people into accepting the white man's religion, churches, history, economics, social decisions and governments as his own! Integration has fooled the Blackman into thinking that what the whiteman has is his also, because that is the law. WHAT A POOR MISGUIDED SLAVE!

1964 Civil Rights Act Prohibits Discrimination

We move into the modern era of slavery and another barrier to the slaves (Blacks) existence; Discrimination. In Asia and Africa, news of the mistreatment of Negroes in the United States had begun to damage the nation's reputation and the whites sought to improve their image by new legislation. In 1964, (100 years later) another Civil Rights Act was passed that outlawed discrimination in all public accomodations, such as hotels, restaurants and theaters. Discrimination by employers, unions and federal programs were prohibited. If found practicing discrimination then federal funds could be withheld.

Keep in mind, that this slave (Blacks) felt that he was free and a citizen during the days of Dred Scott. What citizen of any nation has to have legislation for hundreds of years, constantly beaten and threaten every times he progresses, Identity stolen, discriminated against in all phases of society? What kind of people would do this to another people? What is the purpose? Should blacks continue to seek heaven (money, A good home, and friends) in this white world? No, however Negroes are still Dead!

The first question is white poeple abuse all races of people, ask the Japanese about the atomic bomb. Secondly, the purpose of all this black and white dialogue is Divine, and it is written up in scripture, the end result will be good. Third, black people should stop trying to seek a mental or spiritual heaven in white society, i.e., accepting their names, religion, or unstanding about life. But rather, the knowledge of their own society, culture, and way of life is available today for them if they (Blacks) want it. As for as money, and a good home, they have as much right to the good life as the white man because this land belong to their half-brother, the Indians. The only part of this earth given to the white man (Devil) to live on was Europe, Nothing else.

Joseph, Re-united With His Brothers From Africa and Asia

The Nation of Islam under the leadership of the Hon. Elijah Muhammad is building a nation that will be self-sufficient and not dependent on other nations for its survival except God (Supreme Being) in the person of Master Fard Muhammad. This self rule is what will enable black people to with-stand the famine that is coming to America.

Some scholars say that the famine is a lack of knowledge about the true God; if that is the case then the famine is already here. However, Elijah Muhammad says that the famine will not just be mental or spiritual, but physical as well. The Nation of Islam (Joseph) is preparing himself for a famine in the total sense, with God's help and vision.

In order to rule himself, the blackman must be given a new way of life called Islam. This Islam is not a religion in the traditional viewpoint but rather a Way of Life! In other words, Joseph (Blackman) must practice ruling himself "before" the famine, in order for him to be prepared during the famine. The Nation of Islam must "already" have officers appointed over the land, and take up one-fifth of the plentiful harvest (money), keep food in the cities for storage, and gather all good things together for the famine that is sure to come.

Once the lean years (famine) comes to America, and the Nation of Islam is prepared, then this will draw our brothers from abroad (Asia and Africa) to America, to witness the hand-work of God. To bear witness that this is their long lost brother that was sold into slavery (Joseph) and now by the hand of God has risen to become a ruler in foreign land. Joseph brothers were forgiven for selling him into slavery because as stated in Genesis 50:20 But as for you, ye thought evil against me; but God meant it unto good, to bring to pass, as it is this day, to save /many/ people live. (The other eleven stars making obeisance to Joseph).

The blackman (So Called Negroes) was used by God as a test of Faith to save many people from destruction by proving that he (God) will always come to your rescue, and trials and tribulations plus reward and blessings are all a part of God' plan for the righteous who practice his truth. Also, it proves that Allah is God (Blackman), always has been, and always will be. This knowledge could not be accepted by the human family on Faith, it must be proven and it has been proven. The Blackman Is God of this Earth

The blackman has lived under the rule and control of a Devil for four hundred years. He had his mind taken away and given a negro's mind (a new creation) he was given poison food to eat (Hog), poison drink, alcohol, his religion was taken away, his culture stripped to the degree that he worshiped the devil. He did not know who he was or where he came from. All of these things and more happen to the blackman (Joseph). But it was prophecied in Genesis 15:14–15 And also that nation, whom they shall serve, will I judge: and afterward shall they come out with great substance. 15 And thou shall go their fathers in peace; thou shall be buried in a good old age.

The scriptures has been fulfilled two-thirds; God has appeared in the person of Master Fard Muhammad and the Nation of Islam (Sun, Moon, and Stars) was given as their flag by Allah to show ownership of the universe. The last part of becoming ruler in the land will be brought about by God (famine) and the blackman will be ready to rise to the top, and receive his brothers into the bosom of Abraham. After this experience, the whole world will bear that Allah is God, and he appeared in the person of Master Fard Muhammad, and the Hon. Elijah Muhammad is his Messenger, and the So-Called Negroes of Blackman of America is his chosen people.

Finally, the Bible and Holy Quran always uses symbols and allegorical statements to describe people, places, and things. The Sun, Moon, and stars were to describe Joseph's dream, but the meaning is this: The Sun represent God, and the Moon represent the Negroes reflecting the light or wisdom of God (Master Fard Muhammad, and the Stars represent the other nations of earth bowing down and paying their respect to God and his great work of raising the dead (Joseph) back to life. The Bible and Holy Quran are books of life describing the times, trial and tribulation, heaven and hell, and the rewards and punishment of God's people as told by prophets of God. All the writers of scriptures (Prophets) were black people!

The So-Called Negroes (Children of Israel) Will be Resurrected

The first truth that must be realized is the true "Spiritual Identity" of the So-Called Negroes or Black Man of America. Their spiritual identity in the Bible and Quran is Israel or Children of Israel. If a person reads the scriptures with this fact in mind then there will be a clearer understanding of scripture. The original people of scripture were black and not white. The white man stole the scriptural identity of the blackman and put himself in that place as the people of God. He was able to do this because God (Blackman) gave him dominion over everything on the earth (including scripture) for six-thousand years Genesis 1:26. The seventh day, he must rest; his rule over the people must come to an end. Then God (Master Fard Muhammad) would come and teach the world of the complete truth of what has transpired the last six-thousand years. God is in the world today. This is the whiteman's day of rest, it began in Nineteen fourteen (1914 AD).

That is why this truth of The Resurrection of The Dead is being preached all over the world. It Is Time To Wake Up, And Re-Build The Black Nation The World Over! However, here in America, Israel or So-Called Negroes have been captured, made slaves, scattered over the country (Valley) and they have become so dried (dead) that the Prophet Ezekiel is wondering can these dried bones live? Can they come up out of their graves (mental graves). This is the condition of Israel or So Called Negroes in America! Let us see how Ezekiel described the Negroes. Ezekiel 37: 11–14 Then he said unto me, Son of Man, these bones are the whole house of Israel; behold, they say, our bones are dried, and our hope is lost; we are cut off. 12 Therefore, prophecy and say unto them, Thus said the Lord God: Behold, O my people, I will open your graves, and cause you to come up out of your graves, and bring you into the land of Israel. And ye shall know that I am the Lord, When I have opened your graves, O my people, and brought you up out of your graves, 14 And put my spirit in you, and ye shall live, and I shall place you in your own land; then shall you know that I, the Lord, have spoken it, and performed it, saith the Lord. The So-Called Negroes will be brought out of their mental and spiritual graves and given some land that they can call home. Just as it was before being brought into captivity. Next, God prophecied against Gog and Magog for attacking the Children of Israel (blackman) in their own land. This is what Pharaoh did because he couln't stand for the Children of Israel to go free, and God destroyed him.

Chapter 38:2 Son of Man set they face against Gog, of the land of Magog, the chief prince of Meshech and Tubal. 18 And it shall come to pass at the same time when Gog sall come against the land of Israel, saith the Lord God, that my fury shall come up in my face. 39:6 And I will send a fire on Magog and among those who dwell carelessly in the isles; and they shall know that I am the Lord. 39: 27 When I have brought them again from the people, and gathered them out of their enemies lands, and am santified in them in the sight of many nations, 28 Then shall they know that I am the Lord, their God, who caused them to be led into captivity among the heathen (nations); but I have gathered them unto their own land, and have left none of them any more there. 29 Neither will I hide my face any more from them; for I have poured out my spirit upon the House of Israel, saith the Lord God.

Now who is Gog and Magog that will attack the Children of Israel once God separate them? This attack will cause their ultimate destruction? The Holy Quran gives the identity of Gog and Magogon page 591, Chapter 18, footnote 1525 The ancestors of Gog and Magog are the Slav and Teutonic Races, and in the world-domination of Gog and Magog is thus clearly hinted the domination of the European Nations over the whole world, and the prophecy has thus found fullfillment in our day. So, it is clear that Gog and Magog are God's enemies and if they attack Israel (So Called Negroes) they are going to be destroyed! Finally, Gog and Magog are the European Nations, ancestors of Slav and Teutonic Races, or White People.

The So-Called Negroes were torn down as a nation, stripped of their, Culture, History, Religion, Names, Wealth, God, and Dignity as a people. All of this happened in America, and this is the place where God in the person of Master Fard Muhammad is going to build their nation once again! The vision of Ezekiel' dry bones coming together is how it will take place. The bones (So-Called Negroes) will hear the Word of God because God will blow his breath (New Spiritual Teachings) and they will live. He will put new sinew, and flesh on them (new strength and vitality) and once they began to get strong in God and leave the devil's ways, there will be a great shaking; then it will appear as all of a sudden the bones will come together, bone to its bone. Once the Word of God is breathed into the So-Called Negroes or Children of Israel, and they began to live spiritually, then they are going to stand up upon their feet, an exceedingly great Army; The Nation of Islam! IN AMERICA!

Don't forget, Joseph became a ruler in the same land that he was made a slave. This is the destiny of the Blackman, Believe it or not! Any one tampering with this mission (White or Black) is in jeopardy of being destroyed because this is God's mission (The Resurrection of the Dead Blackman). One of the ways that God chastises a people is Mental; If a person, group, or nation constantly plots against a mission or person that God has selected in his work for a people, then God will cause those people or group or individual to go crazy; so that his work can be complete.

Four-thousand years ago, when white people were disobeying God's laws, they were exiled to Europe where they went crazy and lived the life of animals for "interfering with God's People"; the same thing happened to Nebuchadnenezzar (King of Babylon) who thought that he was God (Same as some white people think today), his Mind went crazy and he was driven from men, ate grass like oxen, his body was wet with dew till his hairs were grown like eagle feathers, and his nails like birds' claws. King Nebuchadnezzar and The Whiteman in the Caves is one and the same. Genesis 3:4 and Daniels 4:33 DON'T ANTAGONIZE GOD AND HIS PEOPLE!

White People Have the World Thinking That They Are the Children of Israel

There are two histories regarding the identity of the Children of Israel. The biblical version gives the identity of the black man, and the history of the Children of Israel from Noah and his three sons; Shem, Ham, and Japheth. These are the sons of Noah and of them was the whole earth overspread, Ham is the father of Canaan. Genesis 9:18–19 (All were black people). The generations of Shem begot Abraham, Isaac and Jacob, and Genesis 32:28 Jacob's name was changed to Israel when he prayed forgiveness for stealing his brothers birth-right; he prevailed and was blessed with a new name. The name Israel means that "he prevailed and was converted to a New walk with God." He was no longer Jacob (a thief) but Israel (a believer) in God.

Genesis 35:6 So Jacob came to Luz, which is in the land of Canaan, that is Bethel, he and all his people that were with him. 35:10 And God said unto him thy name is Jacob: thy name shall not be called anymore Jacob, but Israel shall be thy name:And he called his name Israel. Now the sons of Jacob or Israel were twelve: Reuben, Simeon, Levi, Judah, Issachar, Zebulun, Dan, Naph'tali, Gad, Asher, Joseph and Benjamin. Jacob dwelled in the land where his father Isaac was in Canaan and built an altar and called the place ElBethel. This is how Israel and his people became famous in scripture because he converted to God and established an altar in his name within the very spot that he ran from his transgressions he not only repented but he dedicated himself and family to a new way of life. These were your original Jews or Canaanites from Canaan. All blacks!

The history of the Children of Israel evolves from this point with Joseph being sold into slavery, and becoming the ruler in a strange land, Abraham's seed in bondage for 400 years (so-called negroes) Genesis 15:13 describes the people of the book that are the Children of Israel. White People have never been in bondage to anyone for 400 years. The Blackman must know his Spiritual Identity; it completes the favor that Allah has been developing within the blackman for centuries. Man, Know Thyself!

The other history is that white people claim that they are the Children of Israel; begins in Europe (Caves), when Moses (half/original) brought them out of their misery by teaching, and training them how to be civilized, and taught them his religion, which was Judaism. Moses was a descendant of the original Children of Israel and since Moses was their "spiritual" father, they claim to be the Children of Israel; but Jesus denied their claim in John 8:32 And ye shall know the truth and the truth shall make you free 33 *We are Abraham's seed and were never in bondage to any man. How sayest thou, Ye shall be made free?* 39 They said unto him (Jesus) Abraham is our father. Jesus said unto them, if ye were Abraham's Children, ye would do the works of Abraham. (Jews were never in bondage 8:33 40 But now ye seek to kill me, a man that hath told you the truth, which I have heard of God this did not Abraham. 41 Ye do the deed of your father. Then said they to him, We are not born of fornication; we have one father, even God. 44 Ye are of your father the devil, and the lust of your father ye will do. He was a murderer from the beginning, and abode not in the truth, because there is no truth in him. When he speaketh a lie, he speaketh of his own; for he is liar, and the father of it.

47 He that is of God heareth God's words; ye therefore, hear them not, because ye are not of God. Jesus explained to the Jews (white people) that their father was the Devil, a liar from the beginning, and they were cast in the wilderness where Moses came and raised them up. *Moses became their savior and God. He taught them of all the prophets and the religion of the Gods (Blackman), they accepted Judaism by FAITH, to get out of the caves and to fulfill their destiny of ruling the earth. They are Not Abraham Seed by Nature, but by Faith, BY accepting Abraham's Religion or his way of life.* Next, Jesus come to set the record straight about their ancestry and they (Jews) attempted to kill him by crucifiction, but Jesus did not die on the cross; However the truth that he brought was crucified and distorted.

Eventually, his truth was revised and made into Christianity, which is the Devil's religion, remember that Jesus said they were from the Devil. One thing is certain, white people are not the original Children of Israel but by Faith, the Jews have taken that identity as their own, from the Negroes.

Joseph's Dreams Are Fulfilled in the United States

Master Fard Muhammad is the Supreme Being. He is the wisest human being on earth, thus making him the Supreme Being. He is one hundred per-cent righteous. He is a muslim. He comes into the world to fulfill the scriptures of Joseph's dreams in Genesis 37: 7–9 wherein Joseph brothers sheaves (nations) bowed down to his sheaf (nation), and the Sun, Moon ans eleven stars (the other eleven tribes of Israel) made obesiance to him. The blackman of America is symbolically described in the bible as Joseph. Thus a prophetic fulfillment of Joseph's dreams!

God has said that Joseph (Blackman) will rise in a foreign land (America) and rule; After the four hundred years was up in 1955; Genesis 41 14–32 Then Pharaoh sent and called Joseph, and they brought him hastily out of the dungeon: Pharaoh said unto Joseph, behold I stood upon the bank of the river, and behold there came up out of the river seven fat cows and they fed in the meadows, and behold seven poor, ill favored cows came up and ate the seven fat cows and when they had eaten them, they still looked poor and ill favored. Joseph (Blackman) said here is the interpretation.

Behold, there will be seven years of plenty that will come upon this land (America) and then there will be seven years of famine, and all the years of plenty shall be forgotten in the land, and the famine shall consume the land. (Note: The Sun, Moon and Stars is the Nation of Islam's Flag)

Now Pharaoh (U.S.A.) should understand that this famine is coming upon the land because of their mistreatment of Joseph (Blackman in America). Therefore if Joseph (Nation of Islam) is appointed to supervise the years of "Plenty and Famine" for the entire fourteen years) then America could survive. If not, then who knows what God will bring on the people, one thing is for sure, the Blackman (Joseph) will survive. Another parable of the Bible is when Jesus described the Coming of God as Lighting from the east shining unto the west, in search of a dead carcass (So Called Negroes) that was surrounded by eagles. Read Matthew 24:27. The symbol of the USA is the Eagle. Matt 24–28 Where the carcass is there will be eagles gathered.

The Negro's Mentality is another aspect that God intends to re-make into a Divine Mind. A negro has a mind based on slavery ideas and a false conception of life. It is God's intention and plans to change this Mind into a Mind based on reality. For example, the principle that God uses for growth and development is Ecclesiastes 11:1 Cast your bread upon the waters; for thou shall find it after many days. The So-Called Negroes have not been casting their bread on the waters for Self, they have been casting it upon the waters of white society and it has returned void. This story will give you an idea of what the negroes should be doing.

A negro walks into a bank and ask for a job; the manager informs him that he has inherited a huge sum of money, with one stipulation. He must get a college degree, because the benefactor wants to ensure that his money will be spent wisely. The negro goes to college and gets a degree in accounting in order to spend his money wisely. He returns to the bank with his degree, and the manager takes him to the backdoor, opens it, and says this; *Because you are now educated, you have inherited or taken possession of the ability to go into the world and get all the money that you want! There never was any money set aside for you "UNTIL YOU LEARN TO APPROPRIATE IT FOR YOUR SELF, AND THEN YOU WILL REALIZE, THAT IT WAS THERE FOR YOU ALL THE TIME!"*

This is what the So-Called Negroes of America has failed to realize about the value of Self-production and Self-worth. There is no need to be begging white people for a job, a house, or clothes to wear. If they would pool their resources, energies, and talents into a single minded black-community within the United States like the Jewish Community or Arab Community, then they would have everything they need and more. The problem is a lack of unity and the belief that they can do it. One day God is going to force the Negroes to leave the bank (Whiteman's economy) and go into the world and build for self. Read about Lazarus and the rich man. Luke 16:19 Moral of the story; What you want is in the world, and your problem is learning how to get what you want through developing your talents and skills.

Presently, the So-Called Negroes are stone-headed about doing something for themselves independent of white America. The real reason for this type of behavior is a lack of true knowledge. The foundation of all knowledge is the "knowledge of God and the Devil." This knowledge enables a person to "see" the two systems of life (Positive and Negative), the two nations of earth (Black and White), the two ways of Thinking (Cause and Effect). In reality, there is only one system with two different viewpoint to the same condition. For example, the Blackman of America thinks that he is inferior to the whiteman and is incapable of providing for his needs. But, the truth is that the Blackman has been mis-educated about his History, Culture, and his abilities because he has been restricted from proper development through discrimination, lack of job opportunity, and forced mental slavery, Stone-headed means to Fear Doing Something!

The Blackman was forced to call himself a Negro, and accept a history that was not his, taught false ideas about God in Christianity, denied access to public education, and generally made a second class citizen, thus developing an inferiority complex about himself. As a result of all this mental poison for over four-hundred years, it is no wonder that the Blackman does not want to do anything for himself. HE IS AFRAID OF FAILURE! Fear of Failure is the cause of the blackman not being able to produce for himself. This fear was instilled within the mind of the blackman and woman during slavery and has not left their psyche since. In fact, it is re-inforced through constant talking about the blackman in a negative manner.

God (Master Fard Muhammad) is here teaching the blackman his true history and knowledge of himself. This knowledge will give the blackman the courage and fortitude he needs to succeed and build a society for himself. However, he must have Faith in this knowledge and God. Now, the blackman has more Faith in the Devil than he does in God; this must change! Truth eliminates Falsehood! Good is stronger than Bad and the Blackman will overcome.

How can the Blackman build an "Independent Black Community" here in the United States? What God is calling for is a mental and spiritual separation and not a geographical or land separation. God wants the Blackman to be independent and able to provide for his own needs. In order for this to be accomplished; God has provided us the answer in scripture by understanding Moses and the Children of Israel and how they were led out of Egypt, into the desert, and on to the promised land.

Moses first problem with the Children of Israel was Disbelief; they did not believe that they should have their own Nation. Secondly, God had to punish Pharaoh with plagues like blood, frogs, flies, gnats, stricken livestock, hail and fire. The final plague of death caused the separation of the two nations (Israelites and Egyptians). Once in the desert, Moses started dispensing the laws that the nation would live by, sanctify the first born, eating of unleaven bread for remembrance, (The Children of Israel was in Egypt for four hundred and thirty years). Once in the desert, disbelief surfaced and the Israelites told Moses that it had been better for us to serve the Egyptians, than that we should die in the wilderness Exodus 14:12, Exodus 16:3 And the Children of Israel said unto them, would that we had died by the hand of the Lord in the land of Egypt, when we sat by the flesh pots, and when we did eat bread to the full; for ye have brought us forth into this wilderness, to kill this whole assembly with hunger. Exodus 17:3 And the people thirsted there for water; and the people murmured against Moses, and said, Why has thou brought us up out of Egypt, to kill us and our children and our cattle with thirst? And Moses cried unto the Lord saying what shall I do with this people? (Negroes have been in America for 435 years)!

While in the desert, Moses took the abuse, fed the people, and gave the laws to govern the nation and punished the offenders. The Children of Israel wandered or stayed in the desert preparing themselves for forty years but it was not to be for this generation because their minds were still on Egypt.

Exodus 33:1 Moses was ordered to resume his journey, and go to the land which God swore unto Abraham, to Isaac, and to Jacob, saying to them, *Unto thy seed will I give it.* And the seed of the original Children of Israel went on to build the Tabernacle of God with the Covenant and Ten Commandments and other holy laws to govern the nation The Children of the Children of Israel built a nation under God's Law.

To summarize this story; the So-Called Negroes are the Children of Israel and America is the desert. It holds both Black and White in its midst, and God is calling for a mental, spiritual, economical, and psychological separation. The drawback is that the Negroes love the whites so much that they do not want to separate, so God must send plagues in the form of economic disasters, unemployment droughts, crimes, stealing, and murder. Drugs, Aids, and other are on the way, in order to force the blackman to seek God for his salvation. Once the separation takes place in the mind and in spiritual deeds then the Negroes will grumble, and backslide until they develop Faith in God and his Divine Guidance. That won't take place until much suffering and the manifestation of God's power. After this period, the time should be about (no one knows), then the "Seed of the Blackman" will be Born with a New Spirit of Nationhood, and they will give birth in full bloom to the Black Nation in America. In order for a nation to be born, the people must give birth to another people that will bring this about. God has put it in the hearts and minds of the Blackman and Woman of America to have a nation that they can call their own, and this will come into being. Whatever the mind of man has conceived and believed, it will achieve.

The nation has been conceived and the Industry, Commerce, Business, Transportation and other phases of a nation will be developed. What God is going to do is remove the obstruction that has been keeping the blackman from doing for self; This obstruction can be anything from the whiteman to a stone-headed negro standing in the way of progress. The real Promise Land is mental and Economical being able to live in God's world in peace and enjoying the fruits of your labor from your own tree (nation).

The Promised Land is All In The Mind. It is an ideal situation, place, and eutopia for God's people; A heaven on earth that is based in the spirit of the people. There are no people on earth today that has this Spirit of God within them, including the Negroes. The reason for this is because the Spirit of Satan is still governing the population and his power must be broken before the people can accept a new rulership. Although God is bringing about a world-change in leadership and ideas, it will not take place overnight. In fact, the bible refers to this period as the seventh-thousand years (one day) with God. But, the re-shaping of the minds on earth from unrighteous to righteous is a fact of life. The key to realize is that God is making his government and we should ask ourselves what type of government will it be?

Exodus 19:5 Now therefore, if you will obey my voice indeed, and keep my covenant, then you shall be a peculiar treasure unto me above all people; for all the earth is mine: 6 And ye shall be unto me a Kingdom of priests, and an holy nation. Do you see any nation on earth that is holy? Are there any nations even thinking about being holy? I can only think of one that is attempting to clean up a people and make them righteous; Only one that will put you out of their nation for commiting fornication, adultery, stealing, lying, robbing, and murdering the people. That nation is the Nation of Islam established by our God (Master Fard Muhammad) and his Messenger the Hon. Eliah Muhammad. This is the only nation on earth whose lifestyle is in accord with scriptures.

This nation was born out of the So-Called Negroes of America. So, the Promise Land is in their hands because they are the embodiment of the laws rules, and guidelines set-up by God and his Messenger. A people must represent a lifestyle in order for it to become real. Just as the Children of Israel in the bible represented a God (Jehovah) in that day and times, so it is today that the So-Called Negroes will represent God (Allah) in this day and time with new revelations about the truth and how to live a righteous life. The Promise Land was not just for yesterday, but rather an ideal for all times.

The So-Called Negroes must be reformed Mentally to learn how to Think like Child of God. This reformation is often referred to as the Resurrection of The Dead, because the negroes are dead to the true knowledge of God and how he thinks. What Allah has established for the Blackman and woman of America is a "Spiritual Culture" and this culture has the Divine Knowledge within it to correct their ills. The true meaning of Spiritual knowledge is that this is knowledge from God; i.e. not from Prophets, Man, or other sources, but from God. This is verified in Revelation 21:7 He that overcometh shall inherit all things, and I will be his God, and he shall be my son. (Teach him how to Think)!

Remember, He that overcometh shall inherit all things. Overcome What? God means, he that overcometh Sin in his life. He that reforms from the evil practices in his life. He that stop practicing deceit, lying, cheating, and stealing. He that overcometh this world's life (Satan) and turn to God for help will inherit all things. What does God mean "Inherit All Things". The Kingdom of God is your Mind, and your mind cannot produce the good things that you desire as long as you practice evil. But when you start practicing or thinking good then good things began to happen because your inheritance (Your mind) will give you anything that "YOU Ask For If You Would Only Ask" This is what Jesus meant when he said in Matthew 7:7 Ask, and it shall be given you; seek, and ye shall find; knock, and it shall be open unto you. Believe it or not, everything that a human being receives in this world is no accident, (Because they have been taught how to think by the Devil; Not God).

The thought might have been deposited in their minds unconsciously, or they were unaware of the danger or harm that they were asking for, or through ignorance it happens, but nevertheless the Law of Mind is: As A Man Thinketh in his mind, so is he. First the thought, then the deed. If the black man start asking (thinking) of good, he can reform his own life and start to enjoy some of this heaven like money, a good home, and friends while he live. Once again; Ask (Think in your Mind what you want), Seek (Work on it), and ye shall find (Your mind will guide you to your goal), Knock, (Step up to the task), and it shall be opened unto you. This is the way God Thinks!

The Seventh Thousand Years

The six-thousand years of Satan's rule over the earth (white people) was up in 1914, and now we are living witness that God has made his appearance. This period is a grace period or transitional period for the people of earth as we witness a change in ruling powers in governments. The Blackman will gradually be put back on top, as he should be because he did not decide to give up his land and governments, but were deceived and tricked in order for the Devil to rule as it was prophecied of him in Genesis 1:26 And God said, Let us make man in our image, after our likeness; and let them have dominion over the fish of the sea, and over the fowl of the air, and over the cattle, and over all the earth, and over every creeping thing that creepeth upon the earth.

The seventh day (thousand years) is the day of rest for the Devil or Satan to rule the earth. The seventh day is the "Day of Reality" between God and the Devil. The seventh day is the "Day of Manifestation" in which everything is made known. The seventh day is the day in which the cover is pulled off the devil and his "identity" is made known to the world. God promised Cain that his identity would be concealed and he would be respited until that day (the seventh day). The seventh day is a day of rest from the devil's evil ways and destruction of the planet. The seventh day is the day that Allah makes himself known to the world and it is the day that Allah makes himself known to the world and it is a great day for some and a dreadful day for others.

The seventh day began in 1914 and officially was announced by God July 4, 1930 by the Supreme Being, in the person of Master Fard Muhammad, the long awaited Messiah of the Christians, and the Mahdi of the Muslims. His first revelation was to revealed the cause of all the world's problems and what must be done. He said that the Whiteman was the Devil and must be removed from power to rule over the nations of earth. The blackman was God and must be restored to his rightful place as God of the earth. The seventh day (thousand years) has been in effect for seventy-six years, already there are changes in world powers taking place every day.

In the seventh thousand years all types of slavery thinking must be abolished and the people must be taught how to Think like a God. The people must have a new way of thinking! Jesus said in Matthew 21:43 The Kingdom of God shall be "taken from you" and "given to another nation" bringing forth the fruits of it. To Inherit, means to come into possession of to receive something. The Blackman of America has been given a new nation. This nation is spiritual in its nature and concept; its Constitution or Declaration of Independence is the Laws of God written in Scriptures. It was "given" to the Negroes by God, and taken from the Jews because they have not upheld the laws and brought forth the fruits of righteousness. Read again, what Jesus said to them in Chapter 21 of Matthews.

However, in order for the negroes to accept the Kingdom, and maintain the laws of God, and bring forth righteous fruits; they must be re-made mentally in their thinking and given a new perspective on God and his Kingdom.

Because the negroes have been mis-educated, poisoned, and led astray by the Jews and religious leaders of this world when it comes to the true knowledge of God. They are not prepared to rule themselves or a nation "Spiritually". If they had their own nation today, it could be stolen from them the same way it was stolen before, through tricks and lies, until they learn the "Keys to identifying their enemies." These are mental keys! A key is insight to unlocking a person mind and seeing what is there! A key is wisdom to maneuver in the world without fear of danger. A key is knowledge into peoples nature that identifies who they are (the same principle applies to animals).

The purpose of the Resurrection of the Dead is to put this Divine Understanding into the heads of the negroes. This divine insight, knowledge, wisdom, (keys) will unlock their dead minds or (rusty locks from inactivity) and give them the tools necessary to build a nation. This is the preparation stage, the resurrection stage, the acceptance of the kingdom stage; This is the stage of Lazarus being raised from the Dead; John 11:43 And when he thus had spoken, he cried with a loud voice, Lazarus, come forth.

If Lazarus had been physically dead, How could he come forth? Lazarus is spiritually dead and not physically dead! John 11:11 Our friend Lazarus sleepeth; but I go, that I may awake him out of sleep. Jesus plainly states that Lazarus was asleep; mentally sleep. He was unaware of himself spiritually and dead to the knowledge of the true and living God. The Spirit of God was dead in the life of Lazarus (So-Called Negroes). In order to be resurrected in God, he must believe. The true meaning of Life after Death is that it is a stage in evolution. Just as from dust is evolved the man, from the deeds that he does is evolved the higher man. The purpose of the resurrection is to evolve the higher spiritual man of God. Just as the small life germ grows up to become the man and he does not lose his individuality although he undergoes many changes, so it is that the Man of God goes through many changes in attributes, and grows into that which the person could never conceive of.

Thus when a Man of God raises a person from the dead, it is the evolving of this individual through many stages of higher development to spiritual perfection. This is the meaning of Jesus raises Lazarus from the dead. When this principle is applied to the So-Called Negroes of America; One can see how Elijah Muhammad through the Nation of Islam is raising the Negroes from the dead or from their graves of ignorance about God. The Hereafter is not a mystery that begins after after physical death or beyond the grave, but rather it begins here in this life; For the good people, a heavenly life and for the wicked a life in hell. It all takes place here on earth. Heaven, Hell, Death, and the Hereafter all takes place in this life! There is nothing after physical death! NOTHING!

The reason that is so hard to believe by most people is because they have never really enjoyed life, or understood life, and they say "Is this all? They can't accept it, therefore there must be something else after you die. This belief (Life after Death) provides psychological comfort to endure life's hardships. The blessed are those who know God's pattern of growth or life's cycle; Infancy, childhood, adolescent, adulthood, middle-life, old-age; Then death! This is the cycle of life. Accept it!

What is the significance of a nation's Image to the rest of the world community. A nation's image is its' representation of itself! A nation represents itself throught Music, Art, Religion, Economics, Dress Codes, Ethics, and Morals. All these or any one item can be representative of a nation's outlook on life or protray its image as a nation. The image of the negroes is that of a slave who is still tied to the whiteman psychological in Name, Dress Code, Ethics, Morals, Music, Art, Morals, and in Religion. This means that the blackman does not have an image of himself but rather has adopted his image from the larger culture or white society. He is imagewise a miniature whiteman! A man or nation is only a nation when they are operating from their own God-given Image.

In the beginning, God made man in his own Image, in the image of God created he him; male and female created he them Genesis 1:27 This negro was not created in the image of God but in the image of the whiteman, which is the root of all the problems between white and black. The blackman must get his identity and image back from God so that he can be himself. This is a Divine problem. The Image of God is Righteousness! The Way of Life for God is practicing Righteousness! The only way for the negroes to regain their natural image of themselves is to Think, Act, and Live a life of Righteousness. This lifestyle is in the scriptures. They must stop lying, cheating, murdering and destroying one another and start viewing themselves as people who have been led astray but have returned to their own way.

It makes no difference what or how white people live because they have not been made in the image of black people. The reason blacks do not want to reform and eventually will be force to reform, is because they love white people and their lifestyle. Just like Sampson and Delilah; He loved the women and ways of strange people Judges 14:3 Then his father and mother said unto him, Is there no woman among the daughters of thy brethren, or among all my people, that thou goes to take a wife of the uncircumcised Philistines? And Sampson said unto his father, Get her for me; for she pleaseth me well. And so it is today, with these modern Philistines. Sampson lost his Self-Image.

CHAPTER XI
Blackman's Rebirth: The Blackman Must Be Born Again Mentally First! Then Apply Afrocentricity

Afrocentricity

Afrocentricity is a term used in the black community to indicate that the nerve center for thinking and the origin of black people in America is Africa. It is applied in the school-system to suggest that blacks should be taught Afrocentricity instead of Negro History. The term Negro must be removed and replaced with Black or Afro-American.

The basis of Education is Mind-Development; and if the Minds of the Negroes or Afro-Americans are truly educated, then it must include all of the history of the Blackman, and that means Religion, Culture, Economics, Sociology, and the history of all the races on the earth. After this is done, it will not matter what name or label that describes black education (Negro History, Black History, or Afrocentricity) because the Blackman will be in a through knowledge of himself and could not be tricked into thinking that he is inferior to any other race; because he will know who he is, and that is the GOAL of education: Self-Knowledge.

Eurocentric is a term that has its origin in Europe. The basis of Eurocentricism is a philosophy that the Whiteman is superior to other men of the earth; i.e.

White Supremacy. Most people or scholars think that "White Supremacy is Taught or is environmentally acquired" the Holy Quran says it is Genetic, Holy Quran 15, 3,28–30,31.

28 And when thy Lord said to the Angels: I am going to make a mortal of sounding clay, of black mud fashioned into shape.
29 So when I have made him complete and breathed into him of my spirit, fall down making obesiance to him.
30 So the angels made obesiance, all of them together -
31 But Iblis (did it not). He refused to be of those who made obesiance.

The meaning is clear-that the whiteman has refused to submit to the Blackman from the beginning as being his maker. His Eurocentric philosphy is another attempt to combat the truth of Afrocentricism and the true origin of Man. Did Man evolve from Europe or Africa?

Program for Rebuilding the Black Nation in America; Applying the Restricted Laws of Separate Economics

The essence of rebuilding the Black Nation in America has to be spiritual in nature, therefore any program must began with the Moral Decay within the black community. Secondly, the Economic aspect must be dealt with from a National, State, and local program of Taxation; this income will be used to build the Nation. But, the first and foremost thing that must be done is that God must bring about a separation between the two nations (black and white) so that blacks can see the need for their own nation. The same problem that Moses had with Pharaoh and the Children of Israel; neither wanted to go and build their own nation. Pharaoh (America) was hardened against the idea and so were the Children of Israel (So-Called Negroes) Genesis 4:1 And Moses answered and said, But, behold, they will not believe me, nor hearken unto my voice; for they will say the Lord hath not appeared unto thee.

Once the Blackman is separated mentally and spiritually from the whiteman, then the real work begans. The Restricted Laws of Islam must be enforced to the letter. During the making of "Whiteman" on the Isle of Patmos, there were no prison for criminals because all who were found breaking the law were executed. Crime was eliminated over night. When God's government takes over, there is a good possibility that the same thing will happen again. HISTORY REPEATS ITSELF! The Law is what will clean up Black Peoples Morals!

The Economics are simple because everyone must pay their Taxes, Zakat or Charity to build the nation. It is paid the same way as income taxes are paid within the American Government. The difference is that the money is used for the citizens and the perpetuation of the nation, and not for politicians. The same law applies to politicians that are caught stealing or trying to destroy the nation; Off goes their heads. I realize that this seem extreme to a people that let murderers, thieves, liars, drunks, and every type of people imaginable walk the street and go unpunished for their crimes, but in order to have a safe nation for decent people serving God; THE LAWS OF ISLAM MUST BE ENFORCED TO THE LETTER: Then apply Mercy later on!

Developing an economic blueprint for the Blackman of America is difficult because he does not trust his own people to control his money. A nation's money must be spent to protect itself in every aspect of life. The blackman must learn to trust his own people with his money so that the nation can be built. This lack of trust is why the blackman must be re-educated spiritually in order to open his eyes to the times and what must be done. The united States economy is struggling to keep from collapsing from so much debt and the black will be the first fired; regardless of how many discrimination laws are passed. Here is an outline of what should happen economically.

The Black leadership (Political, Clerical, Educational, Etc.) should form a body of twelve person to act as board to control the black government and the structure should be a corporate structure with officers. Next, they should have a twenty-four person body to control each major phase of industry within the government. These branches of industry would be divided into six divisions i.e. Education, Banking, Technology, Health, Food, and Housing. The six divisions would operate on three levels, City, State, and National. Once the fundamental of government are in place, then taxation must be enforced through voluntary (tax-deductible) contribution to the upliftment of the Black Nation in America." This money must be reinvested back into the building of the nation. Farms must be bought to feed the hungry. Hospitals must be built to aid the sick and destitute. Houses must be built to shelter the homeless. Technology and Banking must be employed to create wealth in the black community. This may sem impossible but it must be done and will be done.

The problem again is in having faith in black leadership to do the job. Although at the present time there is no organized corporate structure in place to get started. Many people are afraid of the Nation of Islam because it is perceived as religious organization for BLACKS only. This government for the Blackman must include all people that are willing to set the blackman on top. All people meaning Righteous People; Blackman must rule himself!

The Blackman's Number One Solution: Separate Economic System!

The Messenger of Allah, Hon. Elijah Muhammad stated that: No nation can be free (Black or White) that does not control its own economics. The Blackman of America or

So Called Negroes have no system in place to save, spend, or control his money in such a manner that it comes back to his community to support his community. The blackman's money supports everybody's community but his own. As a result, there are no black owned and operated hospitals, grocery chains, national gas and oil companies, or any concerns that produce the essentials of life like food, clothing, and shelter.

The Resurrection of the Dead is first mental and spiritual, but then the economics must be put in place because no nation can survive without it, regardless of its nature, religious or infidel. This plan or blueprint is an organizational chart that if followed to the letter will free the Blackman economically and eventually as a nation. Before analying the blueprint, let us ponder on the objectives and why they are necessary. If scriptually, the blackman is "Joseph in the Bible" and he is, then it is necessary that Joseph already have something in place so that he could do business or trade with his brothers abroad.

If a famine or hard times comes upon the land, everyone must eat, and God provides his Elect with the means to feed the people. God does not make everyone suffer, he only shifts the power. At the moment, the Blackman of America is powerless in terms of Economics because there is no system of economic control in place. That is the main problem! He has billions flowing through his hands every year, but he has no cistern for retaining some for himself. The Hon. Elijah Muhammad has provided Divine Inspiration and Leadership to the problem, and once the blackman starts to donate to the Temple instead of the churches, then the Nation of Islam can be built on a solid foundation of economics that is Black Controlled. This will eliminate a four hundred years old problem; Economic Self-Control by Blacks in America, is rooted in his problem of a poor Self-Image.

An Image is the physical, mental, or spiritual reproduction of someone or something. The negro is a mental and spiritual production of the whiteman. The mental and spiritual conception that the whiteman had in mind when he gave mental and spiritual birth to the blackman was that of a slave. He gave the blackman guidelines on how to be a slave. He taught him every phase of life from the viewpoint of his slave. The slave was given ideas about God that were not real. The slave was given the wrong type of food to eat i.e. Hog, also he was fed the wrong mental food about his history (lies). After sixty-four years of teaching black babies these lies, it"sounds the mind" and created a vacuum when it came to self-knowledge and this mental condition is called being Dead, in a spiritual sense.

When the "Mind is Sound" that means that an *impression has been conveyed* to the mind of the negro, that has been accepted! What the blackman accepted from the whiteman mentally and spiritually was his new Identity! A Negro. The Blackman had baceome a Negro. This time frame was from 1555 to 1619, and the reason that they say the blackman came in 1619 was to make black people think that they came here as negroes in Jamestown. Wherein the truth is that it too sixty-four years of poisoning, and training the minds of black babies until after sixty-four years, the whiteman had some black people that had no Image or Conception of who they were or how they arrived in America. From that point on, a new existence or slave existence was developed for the blackman, until the Coming of God, and setting into motion the knowledge that would set the Blackman free, John 8:32.

Remember, the original black people that arrived here in America were not slaves but wise people. They were allowed to reproduce children but they could not raise them; The white man raise them the way he wanted to and he produced "Dead Mind within the Babies". Their minds were trained to love, care, work,and grieve for white people. They also were taught to mistrust, back-stab, fight and hate their own self and kind; this condition is still prevalent today. Love White and Hate Black became their way of life. The negro was made, and now the blackman must be re-made mentally.

(Blackman) Negroes Must Be "Born Again In Their Own History

Who are the So-Called American Negroes? Let us study history and find out. The Cradle of Civilization for the Blackman (Negroes) is the Middle East, African Continent, or the Continent of Asia. The Cradle of Civilization for the Whiteman or Europeans is Europe. The first societies of the world were born along the Tigris, Euphrates and Nile valleys by the Blackman. All of the Prophets of the world (Moses, Jesus, Muhammad, David and others came from this area and was sent to Europe to try and teach White people of Europe how to be civilize but they were rejected. Mathematics, Medicine, the Alphabets, and Numerical system were all imported from the East and carried to Europe in order for the (Europeans) to build up their civilization.

The philosophers Socrates, Aristotle, and Plato all received their wisdom from the Blackman, or muslims. They used this knowledge to establish their educational system and build the City-State. The Europeans use to marvel at the Blackman when he saw his way of life of indoor baths and toilets, sewage system, paved streets, public lights, hospitals and parks, schools and universities. EVERYTHING THAT THE EUROPEANS HAVE TODAY AS A WAY OF LIFE, THEY ACQUIRED IT FROM THE BLACKMAN (So Called Negro). By the way, the Europeans incorporated the word Negro in their language as meaning Black, because when they came to power as a civilization, the blackman's civilization took a rest or died, and Negro means dead to "God Within".

So the Negro must be "Born Again" into his blackness or greatness as a people. The Blackman was the first artist, and some of the oldest drawings and carvings yet to be discovered were drawn by black people (So Called Negroes or white people had not even been thought of in the mind of our people) over 15,000 years ago in Southern France, Northern Spain, Palestine, South Africa, and India. The drawings are on rocks, the carvings on bones; basalt and ivory. This is the true history of the So Called Negroes (Black People) and not Greco-Roman history wherein they are slaves.

(Blackman) Negroes Must Be "Born Again" In Their Own Religion

The Blackman is the father and architect of religion. The oldest and most notable statue in the world bears the face of a blackman (negro). It was erected about five-thousand years ago B.C. and nearly all of the ancient gods were black and had wooly textured hair. In the bible, God, or the Ancient of Days is described as having hair as pure wool, Daniel 7:9. The Bible originated in Ancient Egypt, where according to Aristotle and Herodotus, the population was all black. The social and moral heritage that the Hebrews received from Moses came from the Egyptians (Black People). The Psalms were written by Pharaoh Akhenaton; the Ethiopians gave the idea of right and wrong and thus laid the basis for religion of any kind. In fact, all the ancient worthies that wrote scriptures were Black, including the prophets that delivered the scriptures to different people at different times. All white people ever did was receive, read, and reject scriptures!

Jesus was a half-original man, a prophet, that was sent to white people in Europe to help further Moses' teachings on how to live a righteous life, but he failed in his mission. The quality of righteousness is not in them. Prophet Muhammad came six hundred years later and was inspired with the Holy Quran, which prophecied of black people being lost from their own kind for four hundred years in another religion, believing in another prophet (Jesus) and they must be raised up to the right state of mind or right religion.

Christianity is the white man's conception of religion and they don't practice what they say they believe. Religion is within a people, it is their nature, and the practices are only expressions of that heart felt desire to serve God. Black people are religious by nature, but they are not in the right religion. Islam is the blackman's religion, and God is in the world today to prove it. The house of Christianity is falling because it is built on lies and misconceptions! Come to your own religion and get to know your God (Allah) and see the truth of who the devil really is (Whiteman) and what religion can do for you in this day and time.

(Blackman) Negroes Must Be "Born Again" With Their Own Culture

Culture is the socially transmitted behavioral patterns of the Arts, beliefs, institutions, and all other products of human works and thoughts that are characteristics of a community or people. A people's culture become its "way of life" or habitual manner of living. After being made slaves in America, the negroes made a culture for them selves in order to exist. This culture became known as Negro History or the Negro Experience. This culture has its own "Way of Life" with dietary laws, belief system about God, Devil and society, level of poverty, and institutions that denied the negro the right to marry and raise his own children. They were property and sold as merchandise. This culture existed for three hundred and ten years, and was perpetuated by the whiteman of America.

Now, God has appeared in the land of America, and it is time to give up the negroes culture or way of life and reclaim their own way of life called Islam. The blackman's culture is Righteousness. It is called Islam because Islam is a righteous way of life. In Islam there is no lying, cheating, and stealing from your brother, if caught, then you are punished to the fullest extent of the law. No murdering or slave trading as is operating in the Devil world. The blackman's culture operates according to law and not lawlessness. There are no sex-theaters and prostitution in God's world. That is why the Devil (Whiteman) was kicked out of the Middle East and over into Europe for breaking the laws of the blackman's society.

Once into Europe, he established his own society of filth that has engulfed the entire earth. The So-Called Negroes became a part of it when they were kidnapped, brought to America and made slaves. God warns the negroes to come out of the American culture or way of life in these words: Exodus 6:5–7 And I have also heard the groaning of the children of Israel (negroes) whom the Egyptians (americans) kept in bondage; and I have remembered my covenant, Genesis 15:14. Wherefore said unto the Children of Israel (Negroes) I am the Lord, and I will bring you out from under the burdens of the Egyptians (Americans), and I will rid you out of their bondage, and I will redeem you with an out stretched arm, and with great judgements; 7 And I will be you to me for a people (God in person, Master Fard Muhammad). and I will be to you a God: and ye shall know that I am the Lord your God, who bringeth you out from under the burdens of the Egyptians (Americans).

These scriptures from the bible shows clearly that the culture of the negroes were one of slavery in America, and God comes to remove that condition mentally, spiritually, psychologically and economically by bringing to the blackman his own culture and way of life; Islam. Some black people have become so accustomed to a slavery way of life that they do not want to change and accept God's way of life. If that is the case, then their prodigy will not live through time because slavery is over for the blackman now and forever! God has fulfilled his covenant with the blackman, and all those who do not want to live in their own culture, will go down with the Devil in his culture. The time for the whiteman's culture to thrive is over, it has seen its best days. Hurry onto your own way of life and live!

There are many cultures on earth that the So-Called Negroes could adapt to in order to be raised up to a civilized way of life. However, God (Fard Muhammad) has selected or chosen Islam FOR THE NEGROES, because it completes his favor on the blackman and makes him perfect, or continues to strive for perfection. Islam has no spookism in it, no falsehood about life, no hidden concepts about God or the Devil. Islam is peace! Islam is having money, a good home, friends, peace of mind, contentment, knowledge, wisdom, understanding, living a highly civilized life and not a savage life. The negroes have lived a savage life for over four hundred years and it is time for a new culture (savage means one that has lost the knowledge of one's self and is living the life of a beast). Islam is a voluntary society or culture, and no one is forced to be a muslim (A muslim is one who submits to do the will of God). Once the blackman accepts Islam and starts to build his own heaven here on earth, his own nation with his own people, then there is no limit to the advancement that can be made once he is in his own culture.

(Blackman) Negroes Must Be "Born Again" With Their Own Economy

Economy is the management of the resources, i.e. money, labor or material of a nation. The Blackman of America has no economy to manage his resources so that he can build something for himself. As a result of this lack of an economy to call his own, he is an economic slave to the whiteman. The black man spends billions of dollars each years for food, clothes, housing, and other necessities of life, within the American Economy but he has no voice as to how his money is spent within the black community. In fact, millions of blacks are on welfare, no jobs, ghetto housing, poor medical care, and all of this because blacks do not control their money through having their own Economic System.

Their are no black own and operated hospitals. No Museum to depict our history in a correct manner. No stores or supermarket chains around the country selling our goods and services. No ships on the seas carrying our merchandise to different ports. No trucks on the highways delivering and exchanging products. These things could be done if the blackman controlled his own economy. Why are not these things being done? Because there is a careful plan in effect to make the blackman and blackwoman think that there is no need for a separate economy! Why is there no need for a separate black economy? When black people are dying for lack of medical attention, lack of food, lack of proper housing, lack of jobs, lack of money to live decently; The only reason white people say that there is no need for a black economy is to control the blackman within his economy!

The whiteman has been controlling the economics of the blackman ever since he has been in America. But God (Fard Muhammad) has established a separate economic base in the Nation of Islam under the leadership of Hon. Elijah Muhammad. This economy is in its infancy at the present, but it will grow by leaps and bounds when the blackman realizes that his economic salvation is in jeopardy with the whiteman, and to Build an Economy for Self if he intends to survive the coming world economic crisis.

(Blackman) Negroes Must Be "Born Again" With Their Own God And Names

Negroes have no God because they believe in Jesus Christ and he was not God, but a prophet of God. They do not have their own names because white people stripped them of their names in slavery and still have not given them back so negroes (blacks) are using white peoples names as their own. They have been using white peoples names for so long that they have lost the knowledge of how valuable it is to have your own name. Before coming to America in the holes of ships, our names were Muhammad, Sharrief, Mubara, Ali, or Kareem. These names symbolized our culture and trend of thought as soon as you heard the names. It is the same way when you hear a negro calling himself McDuffy, Polish, Smitz, or Bush, it makes one think of a European, although here is a blackman using the name. It doesn't add up.

The only time it adds up is when one realizes that the blackman has been stripped of his Name and God and it must be restored to him. The bible states it this way in Isaiah 62:2 And the nations shall see thy righteousness and all Kings thy glory; and thou shall be called by a "new name", Which the mouth of the Lord shall name. Allah (God in the person of Master Fard Muhammad) has one hundred names, and he has given the So-Called Negroes the opportunity to accept him as God and one of his name to identify them as the Children of God. (Buy a book on Muslims and African names, and change your name from your slave name to a name of God).

The true understanding of God is this; Your true self is God! 1 Cor. 3:16–17 Know ye not ye are the Temple of God, and that the Spirit of God dwelleth in you? Your body and spirit makes up the God. If any man defile the Temple of God, him shall God destroy; for the temple of God is holy, which temple ye are. Almighty God (Supreme Being) comes into the world to makes these truths plain and clear at the end of the time that Satan was given to rule man with lies and falsehood about his divinity. God is Man manifested in flesh and blood so that he could enjoy his creation; although he is not limited as to how he (God) wish to manifest himself, but for now, if a human being wish to see God, he must look to himself.

Blackman Must Understand His Identity In Scripture, Before He Can Build For Self; Blackman's Spiritual Problem Is Christianity!

The problem with the Blackman of America is that he lacks a true knowledge about God and his religion. The knowledge of God is the greatest and most vital of all knowledge to possess. True knowledge of God is the basis of all belief system or religions of the world. Ninety-eight percent of the people of the earth are without the knowledge of God. A lack of this knowledge is what enables the devil to attract two-thirds of God's people into his religion, Christianity. The essence of Christianity came from Jesus Christ, a righteous man, but the concepts like heaven and hell, life after death, and the hereafter are false. They are designed to enslave the minds of the righteous so that they can be made mental and spiritual slaves to the devil. CHRISTIANITY IS THE DEVIL'S RELIGION!

The inability to answer questions about the universe has cause man to worship his own idea about God. Thus some societies worship the Sun, stone, wood, silver or gold as God. Some even worship snakes, fire and water. They worship all the signs of God as the real God. In this society, many worship the prophet of God (Jesus) as God, this is a real problem! I have mentioned it before and I will mention it again, the Bible tells us how to recognize God in 1 Cor. 3:16 Know ye not that ye are the temple of God, and that the spirit of God dwelleth in you? If the Blackman knew that "he was God" then all of his problems would be over, because he would refuse to bow down to graven image of himself (whiteman) and would go forward and Build for Self.

However, at the present time, he does not know who he is and as a result of this self-ignorance, he is worshiping the devil thinking that it is God. To know God, he must know himself; to know himself is to serve and build for self because this is a form of self-worship because now he realize that God is Within, and doing for self is worship in a true spiritual sense. The creator deposited his spirit in the blackman's soul, and it must be respected, honored, and worshiped through works and thoughts. The negroes are not worshiping God because they do not care anything about themselves, they only care about worshiping the graven image of the whiteman (Jesus wasn't white).

The reason that the blackman's problem is religion is because he lost his identity in religion, he lost his spiritual connection with God in religion, he became blind, deaf and dumb in religion (Christianity) by telling him that God was in the sky and the devil in the ground has poisoned his mind and blinded his understanding about religion. He must be awaken to a true religious understanding of himself and others. When he wakes up, he probably will be angry with the people that blinded him; i.e. Sampson!

There is more confusion over Jesus being alive or dead than any other prophet of God, and I will explain why. The past Jesus's history of two-thousand years ago was a sign of something to come. Jesus was born out of wedlock and tried to resurrect the Jews to a higher understanding of God. Today, Master Fard Muhammad is the Jesus on the scene attempting to resurrect the blackman, who was born out of wedlock from their natural people, but was mentally birthed and spiritually birthed into the world by strangers. This out of wedlock birth meant there was no teaching of their culture, history, religion or even given the correct name. THESE NEGROES ARE Praying, and hoping THAT WHITE PEOPLE LOVE THEM; Blind, Deaf, and Dumb to these last days when God comes to restore the knowledge that has been lost, and unite the nations of the world unto their own kind.

These times are known as the Resurrection of the Dead and the first Jesus was unable to convert the Jews to whom he was sent. On the other hand the second Jesus (Master Fard Muhammad) will convert the whole world because he will open the eyes of the world to that which had been hidden. Some notable individuals that have been raised from the dead and have done great work in the Nation of Islam are: Muhammad Ali (Cassius Clay), Malcolm X Shabazz (Malcolm Little), and Hon. Elijah Muhammad (Elijah Poole) who is spiritually the leader of the Nation of Islam and perhaps the most effective leader of our times. A great man! These are just a few of the great black people that were mentally and spiritually dead in the mud of the white man's world due to his interpretation of Religion (Christianity) that had killed their minds of a correct understanding about God and themselves. They were Resurrected.

The most important Law in Religion is Bible Galations 6:7 Be not deceived, God is not mocked, for whatever a man soweth, that shall he also reap. Holy Quran Chapter 99:7–8 So he who does an atom's weight of good will see it. 8 And he who does an atom's weight of evil will see it. The law of the requital of good and evil is a comprehensive one; Every good deed bears fruit, and every evil deed bears an evil consequence. Regardless to who the person is, regardless to the person's race, or regardless to whether the person is poor or rich; Every man or woman reaps what they have sowen in this life.

The whiteman has deceived the blackman as to who is the real God and has the blackman indirectly worshiping him as God. Commandment number four is: Thou shall not make unto thee any graven/carved/image, or any likeness of anything that is in the heaven above, or that is in the earth beneath, or that is in the water under the earth. He has taken a /supposed/ picture of Jesus that look like him and says that it is God. This suggests subliminally to the sub-conscious mind that God is a Whiteman. He controls the economics, culture, food-supply, clothing, dress fashions and every other phase of the blackman's existence and therefore has put himself in the position of God over the blackman because he refuses to let him "Go and Do For Self" without constant interference. The Whiteman of

America wants to keep the So-Called Negroes (Blackman) slaves forever. He is their God and not Jesus whether the blacks realize it or not. Again, I must repeat, the blackman has been made in the Image of the whiteman, therefore the whiteman is his God.

Christianity has been used as a tool to enslave the minds of black all over the world with its false ideas about life and death. These slave-making ideas (heaven in the sky or a person will be resurrected from the graveyard after they die is shameful). God says that the punishment for mis-leading the world is destruction. The blackman (So-Called Negroes) number one problem is the religion that he believes in; Christianity.

Misunderstanding About the Bible and Holy Quran

The Bible and Holy Quran are spiritual books intended to lift up a people morally by giving instructions that pertain to God. The Holy Quran is a Holy Book whose teachings have not been tampered with since it was revealed to Prophet Muhammad fourteen hundred years ago. The Bible is a religious book but it has been revised and tampered with by King James until the message is not as clear as the Holy Quran's message. However, are the two books used in the Resurrection of the Dead (So-Called Negroes) at this time. The correct understanding of these books will open the eyes of the blind and make known to the world that what God (Master Fard Muhammad) has revealed is true.

The whiteman has the world thinking that God is in the sky looking down on them and that judgement takes place after you die. That is not true! God is Law. Gal 6:7 Be not deceived for God is not mocked, for whatever a man soweth, that shall he also reap. For if he soweth to his flesh, shall of the flesh reap corruption; But he that soweth to the spirit shall of the spirit reap life everlasting. When we speak of spiritual law, it has reference to that which pertains to God on earth, not in the sky. You sow on earth and you reap on earth! That is how the Law of God works. You reap exactly what you have sowed. It is the same law as Cause and Effect, in physical science.

The human Spirit works in the same manner. The law of the human spirit becomes a chain by which man is either bound by good deeds or evil deeds. The rise and fall of man as told in the Bible and Holy Quran is due sorely to his ability or inability to live up to the laws of his creation. The human bodies, communities, and nations are all designed according to the regularity and consistency of God's spiritual laws written in the Bible and Holy Quran such as: Charity, Fasting, Love, Respect, Chastity, Thrift, and the Ten Commandment. The problem arise when people do not want to follow the guidelines of scriptures and then say that they have s misunderstanding.

Dead is a Mental State of Mind

Negro means Dead. The So-Called Negroes are dead because they have buried their talents in the soil of America, and refuse to build an economy for themselves. The parable of the talents is a sign of the negroes. Matthew 25:14 For the kingdom of Heaven is like a man traveling into a far country, who called his own servants, and delivered unto them his goods. One servant he gave five talents, another two, another one; each servant doubled his talents except the servant with one, he buried his talent in the ground. On returning, the master blessed the other two servants and banished the third servant into outer darkness for not using the talent that God gave him. The third servant's state of mind for building was Dead!

Negroes in America are dead to the idea of building something for self based on their talents. The picture that comes to mind is in Genesis 1: 11 Therefore they did set over them taskmasters to afflict them with their burdens. And they built for Pharaoh treasure cities, Pithom &

Raamses. In order to build something for self and use their talents, they would need a Moses (Elijah Muhammad) to raise them from the dead and out of this spiritual wilderness. Negroes are alive when it comes to building for the whiteman because they receive their identity from the whiteman. However, when it comes to building for self, then the mental vision is not there in the mind. Negroes are Dead when it comes to unitying for self! This is a fact. Mental death is the cause of this problem.

Once they acquire a new vision or identity, then they can start to build and use their own talents for self. The problem now is one of identity and not talents. The problem is the Image "Negro" that was instilled and accepted by the slave as his own true self, that must be eliminated from his mind. The "Image of a Righteous Muslim" must replace the "Image of a Negro" in the mind of the Blackman of America before he can build a nation for himself. The real true self of the blackman is a righteous muslim. Negro means Dead. The blackman is dead to the knowledge of his true self, A Righteous Muslim. Negro means Dead and Dead is a mental state of mind.

Is it necessary to talk so much about white and black? Doesn't this disturb the equilibrium of the races? It is necessary because the blackman has been injured psychologically and spiritually, and God is correcting this problem himself, this is Divine Justice. The blackman must receive justice for what has happen to him. There never was any equilibrium between the races; it was and still is a matter of the whiteman on top and the blackman on the bottom. That is not equality! That is slavery! Also, it is time that the world have a new leader because the whole earth is suffering under the rule of the Europeans. It is time for a change! The world has been Dead to what real knowledge, and wisdom can do for them because their governments have been put to sleep with falsehood.

Now, if you are interested, let me tell you how the whiteman gained control of the earth. Revelation 20:5 But the rest of the dead lived not again until the thousand years were finished. *This is the first resurrection. Blessed and holy is he that hath part in the first resurrection; on such the second death hath no power,* but they shall be priests of God and of Christ, and shall reign with him a thousand years.

7 And when the thousand years are ended, Satan shall be loosed out of his prison, 8 And shall go out to deceive the nations which are in the four quarters of the earth, Gog and Magog, to gather them together to battle; the number of whom is as the sand of the sea. 10 And the Devil that deceived them was cast into the lake of fire and brimstone, where the beast and the false prophet are, and shall be tormented day and night forever and ever. 12 And I saw the dead, small and great, stand before God, and the books were opened; and another book was opened, which is the Book of Life. And the dead was judged out of those things which was written in the book, according to their works.

Approximately 1000 AD, the European Nations (Satan) was loosed out of his prison (Europe) to go forth and deceive the nations which are in the four quarters of the earth, Gog and Magog.

Holy Quran titled The Cave, Ch. 18, section 11, footnot 1525. As known in 1523, the anscestors of Gog and Magog are the Slav and Teutonic races, and in the world domination of Gog and Magog is thus clearly hinted the domination of the European nations over the whole world, and the prophecy has thus found fulfillment in our days. The method they (Europeans) use to deceive the world is called tricknology (science of tricks and lies). When the traders lande in Africa among black people, they used Christianity to shield their intentions (making the Africans slaves in their own countries) and said that they were all brothers in God. They should love one another. They said that in their own country there was gold just laying on the ground for anyone that wanted it. They should go there with them to get a sack full and return home. The Aficans got on the ships but never returned home.

This is how they tricked the Indians; The Europeans started bringing gifts, making peace with the natives, and asking could a few of their people come and live among them to get acquainted and learn more of their beautiful culture. Eventually more and more settlers came and began to push the Indians farther and farther off their land. The Europeans introduced whiskey, rifles, and women among the Indians to weaken their resistance. Of course Christianity was used also to make the Indians see that they were "heathens". After a period of time, the Indians were all on reservations and the whiteman had land. The Indians never knew what hit them although the Devil (whiteman) had it planned all the time through tricks and lies or tricknology. In the Orient, the trick is Divide and Conquer. They (Europeans) goes into a nation, VietNam, and tell the dissatified leaders within the nation that they should have a Democracy, and that if they would form an opposing government, that they back the opposition in order to gain freedom for their people. This opposition party is backed politically by the European government and is supplied weapons, money, propaganda material, and sustenance of any kind in order to overthrow the legitimate government in power by the people.

Once the fighting starts, the the European (America, France or England) steps in and says "Let me settle your dispute, don't fight among yourselves because that is not right). The mediator is perceived as a peacemaker and both sides agree to let the arbitrator or peacemaker settle the dispute with some type of agreement. Thus the peacemaker (European) is the cause of the trouble, but he has been able to Divide the two nations as well as Conquer the two nations by settling their dispute. In the Middle East; Religion is the most explosive issue, so they (Europeans) back up financially some Jews to overthrow the government of Palestine, Asia Minor, which at the time, after World War II, was controlled by England or Europeans. They relinquished the government to the Jews, legitimize it in the United Nations, re-named it Israel, and now say that this is the long awaited homeland for the Jews. This is the same scenario that was used to established Kuwait from Iraq.

These governments Israel & Kuwait were established under European rule, and kept enforced by European power and force. They (Europeans) are always in the Middle East trying to get these nations to agree on some settlement. Again, Divide and Conquer! Create the tension, then settle the dispute. You might be asking yourself, Why can't these nations see these tricks? How is it that the Europeans are always able to out-maneuver these nations. Again, we must refer back to scripture for the answer. Revelation 20:5 But the rest of the dead lived not again until the thousand years were finished. This is the first resurrection.

The population of the earth (nations) were dead to the knowledge of who the European were, or their intention of controlling or taking over their nations. Remember dead means mentally dead. However, they would live again, (Become mentally aware) after the thousand year domination was finished. The thousand year domination was finished in 1914. After that began the period of the first resurrection. The first resurrection is known as the Resurrection of the Dead. It is a period where God (Master Fard Muhammad) makes his appearance into the world and explains all things that had been withheld from Man

Some of the things that have not been revealed to Man is the true knowledge of God and the Devil. Who is the Blackman? What should be expected during this transition of world-power? What is the true meaning of Armageddon? Who are God's people? What food should be eaten and what food is forbidden? How should people dress? Is

God a Man or a Spirit? These questions and many, many more have been answered by Master Fard Muhammad, God in Person.

The second coming of Jesus has taken place in the person of Fard Muhammad. Jesus explained it this way in John 14:26 But the Comforter, who is the Holy Spirit, whom the Father will send in my name, he shall teach you all things, and bring all things to your remembrance, whatever I have said unto you. The reason that Fard Muhammad is referred to as God in Person because he is that "Spitit of Truth, that "Jesus" or that "Holy Spirit" who comes in the name of the Father to teach all things. He is the Comforter because this truth removes all aches and pain from the mind and wakes up the spirit. We are living in the Resurrection of the Dead, wherein the world is waking up to the truth and how they got in this condition. The Blackman of America is the first man to be resurrected because he has suffered the most. All nations will rise and God will remove the earth of its burden that has held the world down for so many years.

The nations of the earth have been dead "spiritually" as to Why their is so much confusion until Master Fard Muhammad (Second Jesus) made it plain by explaining God and the Devil, and the Time of transition in which we live.

CHAPTER XII
The Blackman's True Identity is Divine

The Rock

Holy Quran Chapter 15, Section 3, Verses 26-40 explain the creation of the Blackman and the Devil, and the opposition that the devil has in bowing down and submitting to the blackman, his maker.

26 And surely we created man of sounding clay, of black mud fashioned into shape.
27 And the jinn, We created before of intensely hot fire.
28 And when thy Lord said to the angels: I am going to create a mortal of sounding clay, of black mud fashioned into shape.
29 So when I have made him complete and breathed into him my spirit, fall down making obesiance to him.
30 So the angels made obesiance, all of them together --
31 But Iblis (did it not). he redused to be of those who made obesiance.
32 He said: O Iblis, what is the reason that thou are not with those who make obesiance?
33 He said: I am not going to make obesiance to a mortal, whom thou has created of sounding clay, of black mud fashioned into shape.
34 He said: Then go forth, for surely thou are driven away.
35 And surely on thee is a curse till the day of Judgement.

36 He said: My Lord, respite me till the time when they are raised.
37 He said: Surely thou are of the respited ones,
38 Till the period of the time made known.
39 He said: My Lord, as Thou has judged me erring, I shall certainly make (evil) fair-seeming to them on earth, and I shall cause them all to deviate,
40 Except thy servants from among them, the purified ones.
41 He said: This is a right way with Me.
42 As regards My servants, thou hast no authority over them except such of the deviators as follow thee.
43 And surely hell is the promised place for them all --
44 It has seven gates. For each gate is an appointed portion of them.

This chapter was named The Rock because the Dwellers of the Rock are people that comtemplated the destruction of the Messenger and his followers. However, Allah has other plans and he narrates his creation of the Blackman and the destruction of the devil, Whiteman, because of disobedience to his commands.

Allah states that there are two creations (Black Nation and White Nation) operating on the earth at the present time. *The Blackman was created first from sounding clay, of black mud fashioned into shape. The black mud gives the blackman his color and identity as being the first man.* From the blackman, Allah created the races, and the last color is white or the Whiteman (jinn), and he was created of intensely hot fire. The sounding clay, of black mud fashioned into shape shows the characteristics and temperments of these two creations; the blackman is of the earth, and was fashioned spiritually by Allah by breathing into him the Divine Spirit, thus giving him perfection, from dust to perfection.

The jinn, devil, white people are created according to a fiery nature or temperament. This nature tends to lead others to evil, and rebelliousness. They rebel against Divine Laws, whatever God says, "To Do" they say "Not to Do." These two allegorical descriptions of the two nations of earth shows the submissiveness of each nation to the laws of God. The blackman's creation from "Dust to perfection" shows humbleness to divine law and God's way of life. The Whiteman's making was of a fiery rebellious nature and shows rejection of God's laws and way of life.

During the time's immemorial, everything on the earth has submitted to the Blackman, until Iblis, the Whiteman. He refused to be of those who made obesiance. He said: I am not going to make obesiance to a mortal, whom thou has created of sounding clay, of black mud fashioned into shape. Allah said: Then go forth, for surely thou are driven away. This is Adam and Eve being driven out of the Garden of Eden in Genesis 3:24, and Cain Genesis 4:14 was driven out to be a vagabond and furgitive until God comes to execute judgement for the innocent shedding of blood of his brother (blackman). Cain asked to be respited until his time. God put a mark on him (Concealed his identity) and let him loose in the earth. Adam and Eve, Cain, Iblis, Jinn, Devil, Satan, are all names used in the Bible and Holy Quran to describe white people or the Caucausian race. The "fiery nature" leads to destruction whereas the "dust or humble nature" of the blackman leads to perfection.

After being driven out of paradise for breaking the laws of God, Iblis said respite me (give me time to do my work before my Judgement Day; the blackman does not have a Judgement Day, his day of Reckoning is everyday) till the time when they are raised. Allah said, you are respited 6,000 years . The Devil said that he would make every one of earth against God and his laws (Evil would be fair-seeming) or appear to be normal. He would cause them all to fall from the grace of God except the purified ones raised during the Resurrection of the Dead, or Last Days, or Judgement, or the establishment of the Kingdom of God, which would indicate the end of the rule of Satan over this earth.

Allah said to Satan (White people), all of the deviators that follow you, I will fill hell up with them all, because they follow you because they want to. Hell has seven gates (seven spiritually means many ways) and hell is for a portion of time because God comes to save the Righteous and destroy the wicked. But remember, THIS IS A WARNING-----YOU MUST WANT TO BE SAVED IN ORDER TO BE SAVED. Hurry and Join Your Own Nation, the Nation of Islam and Accept your God, Supreme Being, Master Fard Muhammad, and his Messenger, Hon. Elijah Muhammad.

Blackman, Heaven and Hell Is In This Life!

Heaven and Hell begin in this life. The sustenance that a righteous person receives (Not the fruits and sustenance grown from the earth) are not known or realize by the evildoers of this world; They are blind to the peace that comes from one's Soul at rest with God and his Laws. When one's Soul is at rest with God, this is the highest spiritual blessing that one can attain in this life. There is no grief, fatigue, or toil, and the heart is purified of all rancour and jealousy, peace and security reigning all around you; This is Heaven! However, this is not a place for simple enjoyment or rest; it is essentially a place (state of mind) for further advancement to higher and higher stages or states of mind.

Hell is also a state of mind and punishment is not meant for torture but for purification, in order to make person fit for spiritual advancement. The idea underlying hell is; Whomever wasted their opportunity to do good shall, under the inevitable law which makes every man tastes of what he has done be given another chance by under-going a course of treatment (Some people call this a chastisement) for their spiritual diseases. which they have brought about with their own hands. Spiritual diseases are; Lying, Cheating, Stealing, Fornication, Adultery, Murder, Envy, Jealousy and Covetness. It is perfectly clear that when God brings down his punishment it is for our benefit and not to our detriment. In fact, what we are doing is to our detriment and God is trying to save us from our own foolish selves. If it were not for God ordaining a Hell so that we may be saved, we probably would all be dead!

So, Heaven and Hell are two conditions of life for our higher advancement; they become places when we actualize our state of mind to such a degree that we bring into reality. Nothing comes out of the sky except; rain, snow, hail, tornados, or other conditions that come about as a result of a change in atmospheric pressure.

The So-Called Negroes of America cannot mature as a separate nation until they have Power. God in the person of Master Fard Muhammad has come to give them that power. It is Spiritual Power. Spiritual power is power that comes from practicing the Word of God. It is power that manifest as Mind Power. Mind or Mental Power is the greatest power on earth. From Spiritual power or connection with God comes the ability to analyze correctly and understand problems. From Spiritual Power comes the development of inner faculties like Mental Telepathy, Precognition, Visiualization, Conception, and complete Self-Knowledge. Remember, the Negro is dead to "God Consciousness."

Power is the physical, mental, and spiritual ability to do something. It is explained well in the parable of the Talents in Matthew 25: 14-29 The Kingdon of Heaven is like a man traveling into a far country, who called his servants, and delivered unto them his goods. One servant he gave five talents and he doubled it; another two talents and he doubled it; another he gave one talent and he buried it because he felt it was not enought to do anything with. The Lord blessed the other servants with more wealth, and condemned the other servant for not trying to profit with what little talent that he had. So it is with the So-Called Negroes of America, they will not try to build a nation with what they have. They bury their talents in the whiteman's power structure thereby adding more to his already wealthy nation.

The Negroes (blacks) do not realize that as long as they are powerless as a people; economically, then they will be powerless politically and will treated as a social outcast. If the blacks of America separated themselves long enought to build up a power base of money, then it would be easy to get true friends among white people if that is what they want. But, in reality all that one nation wants from another is respect, and a rich nation cannot respect a people that begs for jobs and want do something for itself. Power is not a gift! Power must be earned! Power is acquired by separation, and mutual cooperation between nations of equals. No powerful nation ever shared its power with its slave. The slave (Black) must become an equal through hard work with its own talents and not by burying its talents in another nation. Blackman use your talents to build your own nation!

In order to build a nation for black people, there will have to be a security force or military. The United States has some of the worst people on earth and they are against the blackman being independent. I am speaking about other blacks who are enemies to any idea of self-independence. They are spies and stool pigeons for white people that are afraid to see the rise of the blackman. The military's job is to protect the nation's leaders and assets. also, to enforce the laws of government! one thing that must be made clear is that no nation can enforce laws unless it is on its own land, and that is why it is imperative that the Blackman has some land that he can call his own. Then he can set up his government. This outline is only a sketch to inform you of how it can be done, in a religious government.

Once the military is in place, then the clergy must be established to re-enforce the laws given by God to guide the people. God's laws are intented to guide rather than punish the people for breaking a law.The function of the clergy is to teach the word of God, and is responsible for all spiritual aspects of the nation. In a Spiritual or Religious Government, the Clergy or Ministry is the top leadership, that leads according to the Bible or Quran, Next, the Political leadership that governs the nation; Next, the General Assembly or Parliament that represents the people. Last, the people elect representatives to serve them on the local, state, and national level.ie. Parliament or General Assembly.

It works like this, Remember, God wants a Holy nation, which means a religious nation. First, the people decides what they want in the government, this is conveyed to representatives of Parliament; Parliament votes, and the top leadership (President, Vice-President, Etc.) decides; But now, the final decision is when the Clergy or Ministry decides whether it is in the best interest of the nation "ACCORDING TO THE WORD OF GOD AS STATED IN THEIR HOLY SCRIPTURES". For example, if the people and the leadership wants to sell alcoholic beverages to increase the revenues in the government, and the Scriptures (Bible, Holy Quran or Torah) says "No It Is Forbidden" then it can not be done; The clergy interprets scripture and has the final word.

The problem of the So-Called Negroes is Divine, therefore the solution must be Divine.Divine means having the nature of God; thus the solution of the blackman's problem must emanate or be rooted in God's character or nature. Practically speaking, it must come from Within Self because this is how God reveals himself to the masses of the people. Although he speaks to individuals like Prophets or Messengers from time to time, and through the circumstances of life as he dictates. However, the primary source is through Revelation. The Divine solution written in scripture (Bible) for the So-Called Negroes is the story of Moses and the Children of Israel. If this story is understood correctly and applied realistically to the Blackman of America, then one will see that this is an allegorical picture of what is taken place the So-Called Negroes.

This story has nothing to do with the Jews because they were never in bondage to another people for over four-hundred years (That was the negroes n bondage here in America). The Jews were never "born" in a society wherein they did not know their heritage, culture, or their names.(That happened in America to the negroes). The Jews were never "slaves" to anyone; mental or physical, they have always known who they were (That happened to the negroes in America). The Jews never lost their identity regardless of where they were on earth (That happened to the negroes). The Jews were given a Spiritual Nation in Europe, and that is what enabled them to control the world; they had a superior Spiritual Knowledge of people.

The Jews interpreted scripture in their favor to show where they were the Chosen people of God, and were abused and persecuted for their beliefs. They are the chosen people among white people because they accepted Moses and his guidance. However, the Blackman and another man like unto Moses named Elijah are the actual ones fulfilling the scripture in the Bible of Moses and the Children of Israel. The whiteman has controlled every phase of life including Scripture; Don't you think he would write it in his favor; Just like he re-named the blackman a negro, he re-wrote and re-interpreted scripture to suit himself.

CHAPTER XIII
Colonialism Will Be Broken From Black Nations

Colonialism is a Way of Life for White People

When the white man evolved out of the Dark Ages (Cave Days) into the age of enlightenment (Renaissance), the Muslims had already built beautiful cities in Cordova Spain and Morroco. The Muslims were already building in Europe, and Moses and Jesus had given Europeans a religion to live by: Judeo-Christian, Moses and Jesus were Muslims. White people took this religion and used it as a tool to enslave the minds of the people that they came in contact in Europe, Asia, and Africa. Once the Roman Empire became a world power and under the Emperor Aurelius Constantine (A.D. 306-337) he accepted Christianity, and thus all nations or people under the Roman rule (White) must be Christians. If the Romans captured Carthage or any African nation; i.e. they were either destroyed or made a colony of Rome. This meant that they spoke the Roman's language, their nationality was changed to Romans, their culture became Roman, and their religion became Christianity or Roman. Does this sound like what happened to the So-Called Negroes of America.

    The Romans never intended for their colonies to leave their powers or return to their own way of life. The only way that the colonies regained their soveriegnty is when the power of Rome was broken and could not hold them. Rome was the greatest power of its day, just like America. Colonialism is a policy of extending one's control over another nation. A nation is a people with their own Identity, History, Culture, Flag, Language and God. The Black Man and Woman of America are a nation! THEY WERE KIDNAPPED FROM THEIR ORIGINAL NATION FOUR HUNDRED YEARS AGO AND MADE SLAVES IN ROME (AMERICA), BUT THEY HAVE RE-ESTABLISHED A NEW NATION WITH THEIR SAME CULTURAL IDENTITIES AND MORES IN ROME (AMERICA)

This Resurrection of the Blackman and Woman in America (Rome) is being brought about by a revolution that is going to change the world; A MENTAL REVOLUTION called Islam. The shot that will be fired is--- Colonialism is not the way of God; LET MY PEOPLE GO!

There is a principle in Islam that states; Set free the captured believer wherever you find him. Satan (White people) has captured nine-tenths of the planet earth with his *tale* (Not his T-A-I-L) but his *tale* of Race Superiority and Intellect. Now, God comes into the world to set the record straight as to who is the first Man or God of this planet, Who is the troublemaker? What must be done at this time? What does the Judgement mean? and How will it come about? These are just a few of the many questions that were answered throughout this book.

First, the black man has been captured mentally and spiritually by lies and falsehoods that has been taught him within the Christian religion. Christianity is not for the blackman because it enslaves his mind to lies. There is no Heaven in the sky nor Hell in the ground; Jesus did not originate Christianity, but white people use his name. Whites are not God's people but rather black people are the Gods of this earth. White people have rule this earth for six-thousand years as an experiment in unrighteousness,

(They have done a good job). The purpose in this experiment was to see the dis-satisfaction within the Blackman brought out of his genes in living form. This teaches the Blackman to use his Mind and Inclinations for good only, because he has seen the bad in full bloom. The blackman lost his mental and spiritual identity in slavery!

God in the person of Master Fard Muhammad is the one teaching the believers that believe in his truth. He is the one that is guiding this mental revolution. He is the God of this seventh thousandth year, He is the God and savior of the So-Called American Negroes whether they know it or not. Islam is only one of his method because all truth speaks to this day and his coming. The Judgement could come all at once or daily. With God all things are possible, but one thing is certain, This is a New Revelation to the world and it is setting free the minds of the people that have been captured by falsehood for many thousands of years. This is how the blackman recieved his negro identity in slavery.

First Resurrection of the So-Called Negroes

The name Negro is an inventive of the white man that is designed to separate other blacks around the world and make them think that they are all different it was included in the Latin language meaning Black. It also means Dead! The word Negro indicates that the Blackman, albeit, Jamacian, Nigerian, or American is dead to the knowledge of his real self and origin. It makes the Blackman the world over view himself as different from his brothers; whereas the European Community see themselves as one body (White World). The name was created or invented to divide the Blackman and hide his real identity. For years, nations have been acquiring their names or nationalities from the land mass, or the geographical area in which they live, or from their spiritual identity. There is no such thing as a nation of negroes, in reality, except the ones in America, and that is because they (Black Americans) have been robbed of their identity.

The true meaning of the Resurrection of the Dead is for the So-Called Negroes to be raised up into the knowledge of one's identity, culture, nation, religion and God. Religion is the division of life into two separate division; heaven and hell. If one possess the knowledge of Self, God, and Others, then that is heaven. The absence or ignorance to that knowledge signifies hell for that person or nation. The negroes are in hell because they lack this vital knowledge of Self. The First Resurrection is designed to impart the true knowledge of Self to the negroes and thereby bring about an understanding of himself.

The First Resurrection is mental and spiritual, and the laying of the foundation on which to build a nation. The pattern of building was established by the Messenger, (Hon. Elijah Muhammad). The Laborers that believed in his work, must carry on that work in the same manner and spirit. First, develop a spiritual base by teaching Islam the same way that the messenger taught it. Second, Teach and train the believers our culture, and third establish some businesses or economics of our own.

The Blackman of America (Muslims) are building a nation and not just establishing Islam here in the West, because religion (Islam) is a vital part of our nation like Education, Economics, or Politics. It is the base from which we build our nation. The minds of black people in America must evolve from that state wherein the Muslims are only viewed as a religious organization. The Muslims (Nation of Islam) or So-Called Negroes are being raised to the idea of their true destiny, and this is the second stage of that resurrection. *The second resurrection means to build on the foundation that has has already been established by the Messenger! "Raising the Consciousness of the negroes to a Godly level."*

The Islamic foundation for the So-Called Negroes is: *Change your Name* legally from the whiteman's name to one of God's names or attributes. Names represents ownership and as long as black people are using white peoples names it indicates that they still own black people (Spiritually if not Physically). Next, *Get out of Christianity and into your own Religion, i.e. Islam.* Christianity is taught in such a way that it makes black people slaves all over the world by showing that they are inferior and white is superior because all the Prophets and People of God are white. *Change your Dietary Laws* and stop eating the Hog immediatedly! *Love and Respect your Black brothers and sisters.* Support your nation (Nation of Islam) and *build an Economy for yourself* to protect you against the day of want that is surely coming upon America. It is in the wind, just listen and you will hear the rumbling on Wall Street and in the White House.

Read Chapter 21 of the Bible concerning the Coming of God and the establishment of the Kingdom! Therein are the ideas and concepts that the believers are to live by and practice as a nation of people. They are not theories but facts of life. First, God must come, then the Messenger to teach what God has taught him, then the believers must build on what the messenger taught them about, The entire process is Building A Nation and it is spiritually called the Resurrection of the Dead.

CHAPTER XIV
The Final War: Regaining the Blackman's Birthright, Economy, and Moral System

The Last Message; John 8:32 Ye Shall Know The Truth and The Truth Shall Set You Free

Revelation 22:12 And behold, I come quickly, and my reward is with me, to give every man according as his work shall be. The first resurrect was the laying of the foundation by the messenger (Elijah Muhammad); and the second resurrection is the building on the foundation that the messenger laid down for the believers; and the third stage or resurrection will be to give each according to his works. If the Blackman or Negroes refuse to build a nation for themselves and continue to rely on the whiteman for his sustenance then when his government falls, the negroes will fall with him. Each nation will be rewarded according to its deeds. If the blackman has no nation and is practicing the same habits and ways of the whiteman, then he will be given the same rewards. This Is The Last Message To Come To The Negroes To Stand Up And Be A Nation, It Is Called Islam, Take It Or Leave It; It Is The Truth.

The Holy Quran states the Last Message in this manner, The Kneeling, Section 4 The Doom 45:28-29 And thou shall see every nation kneeling down. Every nation will be called to its record. This day you are requited for what you did. 29 This is our record that speaks against you with truth. Surely we wrote what you did. The record or book that each individual or nation is called into account for is his own actions . On the Day of Resurrection, the effects of a person's deeds will be revealed to its fullest. A person's evil deeds are like unto a prison because it hampers his progress and keep his faculties shut up from doing great and good deeds. Whereas the person whose book or record is of good deeds will find himself in the highest places because by good deeds the faculties given to man find their highest development.

That each nation has a book bears out the truth that the impression of what a people do is left on their national life, and nations like people are judged for what they do; "Lo! Read my book" (69-19) The evil-doer is made to say: "O would that my book had never been given me, and I had not known what my account was! The evil that was done to the blackman and woman of America can never be fully repaid, but the main reason that God came to the So-Called Negroes was to restore their Identity. If their true identity (Original People of the Earth, Originators of the first Civilization, Developers of all the Sciences used by man) is not accepted and acted upon; then it would be useless to build a nation because they still would not know who they really are. The knowledge of Self or Knowledge of your own Identity, is the first step in being a civilized person or nation. A nation can't be built without an Identity.

That is why the teachings of Islam is so important to the Black Man of America because it gives him his identity. No other science, religion, or history is as complete in giving the So-Called Negroes what they need as Islam; taught by Hon. Elijah Muhammad. There are many versions of Islam being taught in America and the world, but they do not teach the blackman his identity as the Hon. Elijah Muhammad. If a person listens to Islam and accept his identity mentally and spiritually, but do not act upon that knowledge physically; i.e. stop eating hog, drinking alcohol, stop fornicating or commiting adultery, stop lying and cheating, change your name from the slave name to one of God's name; if these things are not done after hearing Islam mentally, then that person is still a negro. The term that applies is: The words have been accepted mentally but they have not penetrated to the heart.

Blackman, in order to build a nation for yourself, the words must be accepted mentally and spiritually until the words penetrate to your heart and gives you a new identity; A Muslim Identity or A Muslim Mentality. With a muslim mind or muslim mentality, then and only then will the negroes be qualified to build a muslim nation, the Nation of Islam. Allah does not intend for the blackman to build a hog eating, wine drinking Negro Nation of black people. We must accept Islam in our hearts until the Mind becomes Islamic in nature, and Divine in spirit. That is our purpose, our goal, our desire, and with the help of Allah it will become our destiny. Every man or nation will be rewarded according to his works. BELIEF COUNTS FOR NOTHING UNLESS CARRIED INTO PRACTICE!

In this book, Spiritually, NEGRO MEANS DEAD, it is based upon the past, present, and future outlook of the So-Called Negroes in America. The valley described in Ezekiel's vision 37:1-10 depicts how dead they have become as a nation and the Son of Man (God in Person, Fard Muhammad) starts blowing the wind (Islam) upon the slain minds of the negroes so that they might live. The trumpet that is sounding in their deaf ears is Islam. The grave that they are laying in is Christianity They must be raised from the false concepts in Christianity that has killed their understanding about life. This is known spiritually as being "raised from the dead to a Divine level of Thinking."

The restoration of the House of Israel or the Children of Israel is done by the Hon. Elijah Muhammad, Messenger of Allah. It is the Hon. Elijah Muhammad that established the house known as the Nation of Islam to restore the negroes's national heritage, identity, religion, culture, names, and a correct understanding of God and the Devil. He is the one that converted the Children of Israel or Negroes from their transgressions and sanctified them in the sight of many nations. He is the one that laid an Islamic Foundation for the Negroes to build a New Nation! They do not need anyone's approval or sanction because they have God on their side. All that must be done is to come together in this valley of America under the Flag of Islam and practice nationhood.

The dry bones in the valley represents a dead nation within another nation that must be resurrected by God and his messenger. The people have been slain and scattered all over the valley until they had no flesh and had become bones. God restored them back as a nation by teaching the truth of their religion, Culture, and God. The Children of Israel had to be taught of the enemy that put them in that condition so that they would not fall prey to them again. The Hon. Elijah Muhammad is the greatest man that has ever lived (besides God) because he has restored the dry bones back together as a nation (Nation of Islam) to live forever. Long live our God, Master Fard Muhammad for coming and giving us life; When we were Dead in our graves. Restoring our identity and names. Negro is dead state of Mind a "Frozen Embryo" in a womb and cannot function for itself until it is born. This state of mind is what enables the blackman to be called a negro, because he is unable to do for self until freed mentally and spiritually by God. The Truth of Islam is what will free him.

The main problem with the Blackman remaining a Negro is "Fear" that was instilled in him when he was a baby in slavery. The whiteman put fear in the blackman as a child, and this condition is perpetuated as a man by teaching the blackman to eat the wrong food. The wrong food is mental as well as physical food. The mental food is a false history of who the blackman is, wrong concepts about God and the Devil, wrong ideas about how and when civilization started. No education of any kind for over four hundred years. The wrong physical foods are items like the Hog, collard greens, Large lima beans (too much gas), and alcohol and other intoxicants. Also, Cigarettes, snuff, and other drugs. This mental and physical poison has destroyed the blackman's spiritual conception of himself as a Child of God.

The destruction of the Blackman's conception of himself is the root of the problem and the reason why he cannot get up and go for himself as other nations are doing. The first thing that God in the person of Master Fard Muhammad is doing is restoring the Blackman's mental and spiritual conception of who he is. The blackman has lost the knowledge of who he is through accepting the identity that the Devil gave him, which is FALSE IDENTITY CALLED NEGRO. The knowledge of Islam will eliminate that confusion within his mind if he will only Believe, then act on that knowledge. Negro is only a state of mind. I repeat, NEGRO IS ONLY A STATE OF MIND THAT MEANS DEAD TO THE KNOWLEDGE OF WHO YOU ARE. It is not the blackman's nationality or origin, it has its roots in the whiteman's world and is a term he uses to apply to black people. No black nation on earth has ever called themselves Negroes before the whiteman started Name-Calling other nations all over the planet.

The blackman by nature is a righteous muslim, and in order for him to regain his identity, he must accept Islam and the be himself.

A person's name or "spiritual identity" is the first ingredient necessary in the building of their culture, heritage, religion, or economy. A person's name or "mental identity" is their conception of themselves. A person's mental conception of himself may not be the same as their spiritual identity. This causes conflicts within the individual or nation because the two identities do not add up or balance the nation or individual. For example, the black man's spiritual identity is of God, which is all powerful and creative. However, through tricks and lies, his mental identity is that of a Negro, a powerless dependent nation which relies totally on the white man for survival and sustenance. What is wrong? If he is from God and has a creative mind, then why don't he create a nation to provide for his own needs? He doesn't know his identity

That is the purpose of this book, to indicate that the blackman has been robbed of his spiritual identity and don't know who he really is; thus, the new mental identity that was imposed on him in slavery is the only identity that he knows. He must be throughly re-educated into the knowledge of his real self. His real self is a righteous muslim. He is not a negro. His nation must be re-built because he was robbed and kidnapped and God promised to bring him out of this condition with great substance. He will build his nation on the very soil wherein he was a slave. Read about Joseph' rise within a foreign land. The dry bones coming together and building a nation. The rich man died and the slave Lazarus was taken to heaven in the bosom of Abraham.

THE FIRST THING THAT THE BLACKMAN MUST DO IS CHANGE HIS SLAVERY NAME TO A DIVINE NAME OF GOD; AND THERBY CHANGE HIS MENTAL AND SPIRITUAL OUTLOOK ON LIFE! Once the blackman knows himself "spiritually" then he can re-align his mental identity with with his newly acquired spiritual identity. Example; Spiritual Identity is a muslim, Nation is Nation of Islam, Language is Arabic, God's name is Allah, Negro's name was John James and now is John Muhammad. The spiritual identity now is in accord with the mental identity. The restoration of the spiritual and mental identity of the blackman is the Resurrection taking place today. Blackman, Negro Means Dead!

Brothers and Sisters, I realize that it must be a shock to your Emotional system to think that this is the "Truth" that Jesus was talking about two-thousand years ago, (The truth that will set the Blackman's Mind free from being captured by the Devil's lies and deception). The truth of who is God and the Devil? What must be done after Lazarus (Negroes) are raised from the dead? Has Jesus reappeared in the person of Master Fard Muhammad? Is Elijah Muhammad really a Messenger of God? Remember this, Messengers of God like Moses, Jesus, or Elijah Muhammad are always spoken of as being alive because their Truth lives on in the people. The Blackman and Whiteman are the two main characters spoken of in the Bible and Holy Quran, but they are spoken of in allegorical terms and in parables so that their identities will not be known until a Divine person reveals it; like a Prophet or Messenger.

The Blackman had to be put to sleep mentally with falsehood about his identity in order for the Whiteman to rule the planet earth for the last six-thousand years. If the Blackman was still in the knowledge of who he was Divinely (God), then there was no way that the Whiteman could have ruled and therefore the Scriptures could not have being fulfilled Genesis 1:26 And God said, Let us make Man In our Image, after our likeness; And let them have dominion over the fish of the sea, (Remember, let "Them" have dominion), and over the fowl of the air, and over the cattle, and over all the earth, and over every creeping thing that creepeth upon the earth.

This is the Truth that Jesus was talking about; This new man was given dominion over all the earth, including the Nations Minds and their Way of Living. He altered every nation on earth lifestyle and Way of Thinking. He gave them a new Way of viewing life other than their original way. This New way is called Unrighteousness; meaning that whatever God said "Thou Shall Not Do", He said "Thou Shall Do." Jesus in John 8:44 told these New People" that were new in their ways and habits of not serving God "Ye are of your father the Devil, and the lust of your father ye will do. He was a murderer from the beginning (Cain slew Abel) and abode not in the truth, because there is a liar, and the father of it. Now, let's explain the purpose of making this new Man to rule the earth for six-thousand years. The purpose of White people was to lead the world astray from Righteousness into Unrighteousness, so as to prove that God does reside within Man and that Man (BLACKMAN) was created in Righteousness, and that he is the God and Owner of this earth, and was able to be be subdued and controlled for six-thousand years; but would rise up in one day (a thousand years) and reclaim his home and prove that he is God and always will be of this earth. It is unrighteousness that keeps White People in control of Black People! This is explained in the parable of the tares being sown in with the wheat. Matthew 36:43

Jesus explained to his disciples the parable of the wheat and tare. 37 He that soweth the good seed (Jesus) is the Son of Man (Truth) 38 The field is the world; the good seed are the Children of the Kingdom, but the tares are the children of the wicked one; 39 The enemy that soweth them is the Devil; the harvest is the end of the age (six-thousand years) and the reapers are the angels. 40 As therefore, the tares are gathered and burned in the fire, so shall it be at the end of this age. The Son of Man shall send fort his angels and they shall gather out of his kingdom all things that offend, and them who do iniquity. 42 And cast them in a furnace of fire there shall be wailing and gnashing of teeth. 43 Then shall the righteous shine forth as the sun in the Kingdom of their Father. Who hath ears to hear, let him hear.

The Blackman of America does not realize that the good seed that is being sown today is the Truth that will set him free from four-hundred years of deception about his identity. The Son of Man that is sowing these seeds is Master Fard Muhammad, the harvest is the So-Called Negroes, and the New Kingdom that is chosen for the Blackman is the Nation of Islam. Once the blackman began PRACTICING ISLAM, he will began to shine forth as God intended. He who has ears to hear, let him hear.

These are some of the truths that the Blackman must know and be accepted --- as the truth; in order to be free mentally and spiritually, he must know the real truth about himself and the whiteman, concerning his History, Names, Religion and their creation. The Blackman is the first Man and the creator of all other men or races. The Blackman built the first civilization, developed the laws of Right and Wrong, and created Religion as a science to live by and serve the Almighty God which is a power that dwells within his own being (Mind). He is Self-Created in triple darkness and manifested in flesh and blood from a small life germ that animated in space. He always was there and the phrase "Once upon a time" is appropriate to describe his beginning. His creation is the universe, and his home is the planet earth. The universe is constantly revealing itself by manifesting unknown planets in space, the last was Pluto or Platoon. That is why God could not be beyond the Sun, Moon, and Stars because there is nothing outside of the universe but outer darkness.

All life is within the universe, regardless of its form or shape, it is within the universe. Now to the planet earth. Each planet produces its own food and substenance for the inhabitants of that planet. The earth produces oxygen, food, clothing, material for shelter, and the Blackman produces knowledge from within himself to instruct himself on how to live and thrive on his own home. The Blackman nor any other creature on the planet earth can leave and go live on another planet, this is their home. This was proven by the space exploration to the Moon. When the astronauts went to the Moon, they had to take everything that they needed to exist with them like food from earth, oxygen to breathe, because none of this material or ingredients exist in the same form as our planet. This tells the human being that he will not go and live in another place after he dies on earth, because his destiny is to live and die on earth! That is his cycle of life.

The Devil lied to the Negroes and they must be Set-Free from this deception of what takes place after they die. Within himself, he must BELIEVE IN HIMSELF. His mind operates in such a manner that whatever he accepts within himself whether Truth or Falsehood, it is manifested in his daily life as truth and becomes a part of his being. That is why it is so important that he accept truth because he was created in truth, and whatever he accept will become a part of his life (true or False). If he accepts lies in his life (as the truth) then his mind can make a lifestyle out of a lie, to the extent that he won't know it is a lie himself (the term is Self-delusion). Self-delusion is a false belief held by an individual or people in spite on invalidating evidence. Which brings us to the point of how the Blackman came to view himself as a Negro.

After being captured physically by the whiteman and brought into slavery, the whiteman put a mental chain on the brain of the blackman that exist today; he changed the blackman's identity! He told the blackman's offsprings or babies that they were savages from monkeys, and were swinging on trees in Africa. He rescued them and brought them to America to civilize them to a new way of life. He told them that they were Negroes which meant black (all lies). He beat them from morning to night, lynch them on the week ends for sport and play, made homosexuals of them, made drunkards, kept them from any form of education by law for over 300 years. Refuse to let them marry and this bred fornication, AND LACK OF LOVE FOR THE FAMILY STRUCTURE, this is still prevalent today. This way of life was accepted by the blackman Mentally in order to survive. Remember, the blackman accepted this mentally although he was taught lies.

The Whiteman was the one swinging on trees in the caves and hillsides of Europe (Read about the caveman in your history books). The blackman was the one who drove the whiteman into the caves 4,000 years ago, Genesis 3:24

and he made the Blackman's descendants negroes as a act of revenge. The negroes are deluded by thinking that their origin or nationality is negro. There is no such thing as a blackman being an original negro by birth except in America because Negro means being dead to the knowledge of yourself. Not Your Origin or Nationality. The Earth is the home, origin, and nationality of the Blackman!

Slavery names that originated from the whiteman must be abolished immediately before the Mind of the blackman and woman can be set-free. Remember, the time in which we live is the time spoken of in Genesis 15:13-14 wherein God spoke to Abram, Know of surety that thy seed (Spiritual seed or God's people) shall be a stranger in a land that is not theirs (Remember Dred Scott found out he was not a citizen) and shall serve them; and they (White people) shall afflict them four hundred years; (Slavery) 14 And also that nation (America) whom they shall serve, will I judge: and afterward shall they come out with great substance. This scripture has been fulfilled to the letter except for the blackman coming out with great substance. That is being fulfilled right now as the blackman practice Islam and remove himself from the lifestyle of the whiteman, AND MOST OF ALL GIVE HIM BACK HIS NAME AND RELIGION CHRISTIANITY.

The blackman must get his own righteous black name and lifestyle. He must give up Christianity because that is what keeps him a spiritual slave to the whiteman's conception of life and God. Once he has his History, his own Religion Islam, and his own name and living up to the moral precepts of that name, then he is free! He will never be free as long as he is satisfied with being lost in another man's identity and culture. Is the blackman waiting for the whiteman to tell him these things? That day will never come! No captor in the history of the world has ever told the people that they enslaved that "It is time for you to rise and rule yourself and the world, we are sorry that we mistreated you for four-hundred years, and took away your

Land, Name, Heritage, Language, God, Money, Dignity, Identity, and your Conception of Life, but that is all over with now, so forgive us and everything is forgiven. That has never been done and it never will be done now!

However, here is something that could happen with God's help. The people that accept Islam, change their Name and reclaim their Religion, Heritage, Culture, Identity and everything else that was taken mentally and spiritually could be offered a substantial amount of land to live their own way of life, and enought money to support themselves (Muslims) for twenty years until they are self-sufficient as a nation. This would go a long way towards removing some of the injustices done to the blackman while here forcibly in America. Consider this Law of God "Be not deceived for God is not mocked, whatsoever a man soweth, that he shall also reap. Galatian 6:7" America is going to pay for what she has done to the blackman and woman. It is not up to the blackman to forgive and forget, because this is a Divine Law working in nature and it must be carried out. But good deeds are not overlooked either, and this plan of Reparation that I mentioned will ease the pain of re-establishing the black nation that was destroyed here in America.

If it was in the hands of the blackman of America to forgive the past deeds of the whiteman, and remain a slave lost in this culture; he would do just that because he loves his and master and any thought of uniting with his brother is repulsive. That is why God is instilling love between the blackman and his brothers, at home or abroad. For the first time, the blackman in the Western world has sympathy for his brothers in the East Africa), and this is because they both have been bitten by the same beast. The only difference is that the African is fighting to regain his homeland and the Blackman in America has to totally rebuild himself a home; but do not fear because God is in the plan.

Didn't it ever cross your mind how things got like they are in the first place. Isn't it strange that a Blackman can produce a whiteman, but yet the whiteman is ruling the producer? How did this happen? The scriptures are the only souce of revealing the truth. But, it takes God or one of his representative to unravel this strange and penetrating knowledge of Man. The average individual will not spend the time and effort to understand the word of God, that is why he sends teachers like Abraham, Moses, Jesus, Fard Muhammad and Elijah Muhammad. After this truth, there will no need for another teacher, because MAN WILL KNOW HIMSELF! That is the purpose of these teachings, to answer the questions of man down through the ages of Who Am I? That has always been the question and now we know the answer, thanks to Master Fard Muhammad and Hon. Elijah Muhammad; Man Is God! This is the Truth that wil Set-Free the stone-head of the Blackman.

Finally, let us not forget the three steps that ARE REQUIRED for the complete "Resurrection of The Dead (So Called Negroes of America). The first step is; (1) The First Resurrection is the Negroes or Blackman must be throughly re-educated back into the true knowledge of his Identity, Ways of the Devil, Culture, History, Flag, Nation, and his God. Only then will he be qualified to build something for himself; Self Education is first!

(2) Blackman's "Image of Self" must be changed from a Negro back to his original Image, which is the Father of Civilization.Once his Self-Image has been re-established correctly, now he can start to build on the right mental foundation. Romans 12:2 And be not conformed to this world, but be ye transformed by the re-newing of your mind, that ye may prove what is good, and acceptable, and perfect, will of God.

(3) The Second Resurrection of The Dead is the third stage of this evolution or Resurrection of the Blackman. This is the building stage where he must A. Change his Name from the Whiteman's name to one of his own African or Muslim names. B. Change your Dietary Laws and

stop eating swine. C. Accept your own Religion, Islam. D. Build your own Economy. E. Love your Black brothers and sisters. F. Support your Nation and recognize its Flag, the Nation of Islam.

Accept your God and his Messenger that have come to make you an independent people (Master Fard Muhammad and Elijah Muhammad). Once again, the three steps of the Resurrection are: Re-education of the Blackman, Changing his Self-Image, and Building on those two mental foundation a New Nation in America of Black People that will become the foundation for the new world of God scripturally called the Kingdom of God, and referred to as A New Heaven and New Earth (new Mind and Body). Revelations 21:5 Behold, I make all things new. And he said unto me, Write; for these words are true and faithful.

Just as sure as these words are written, a "Depression" is coming upon America because of her reckless spending (Joseph in Pharaoh's Government). The black leaders of this nation should organize and develop a "Corporate Structure" of twelve people with a Board and Officers. Next, there should be twenty-four Cabinet members assigned to each major area of the economy. These twenty-four areas should be divided into six major divisions like; Food, Health, Technology, Shelter, Clothing, and Banking. These six divisions should exist on all three levels of government, i.e. Federal, State, and Local. The people should be taxed voulontarily like the "Black United Fund" in order to get the resources to buy land and start growing food for the coming depression. They should start setting-up local First-Aid stations for the poor in the inner cities, They should start building pre-fab housing as an example of what can and must be done to fulfill the scriptures of feeding the hungry, clothing the naked, and making the blind to see. This is the Blackman's Job in The Second Resurrection of the Dead. TO "BUILD" A WORLD FOR HIMSELF; SO THAT WHEN THIS GOVERNMENT COLLAPSES BECAUSE OF EVIL AND INDECENCY,

HE WILL BE ABLE TO SURVIVE. Because of certain similar Spiritual conditions that exist within the United States, it is often compared to ancient Babylon and the Roman Empire (Empires that fell because of evil and indecency)!

The Last Message, Holy Quran 45: 28-29 The Doom And thou shall see every nation kneeling down, every nation will be called to its record. Give every man according to his works! Nations and Individuals reap what they have sown in this world and not after they physically die! AIDS IS ONLY ONE THE PLAGUES THAT GOD WILL USE TO TURN THE POPULATION AROUND TO PRACTICING RIGHTEOUSNESS ONCE AGAIN ! Hurry, and get your life in accord with the Laws of God!!! Being a Devil means living a wicked lifestyle, and being a God means living a righteous lifestyle. The War of Armageddon only means which Way of Life will you chose in these last days; i.e. God or the Devil. The choice is up to you! IT IS TIME TO SEPARATE MENTALLY AND SPIRITUALLY BETWEEN BLACK AND WHITE ! Physically Let each nation live according to its own Identity; That is what God wants today for the people of earth.

The Blackman of America is extremely blessed to have Master Fard Muhammad to come to them personally and give them Divine Wisdom to live and be guided by during these troubled times. Being a Man, I cannot say if he is stiil alive physically or not but that is not the point because Spiritual people never die; they live on in God's wisdom and the people. He will always live in the hearts and minds of those (like myself) who has accepted his truth and vision. Also, the world is conforming to his Truth of change and destruction; like Communism downfall and the rise of Islam in America and throughout the world. Democracy will stand as a principle but the Economics of the haves/ have-not structure of providing for the peoples well being must go. God says America will be destroyed and it will be! I do not know if he means the Power Structure that rules this country, the Economic System, or the Racism that controls blacks.

I have accepted God version and view point of the world. He said that the Blackman was created first and that he was created from Dust, which means a humble origin and his nature was temperate (moderate). As opposed to the creation of the Whiteman, whose nature is fiery (rebellious). Those allegorical types of description shows that the Blackman is submissive to Divine Laws and the Whiteman is rebellious against them. It indicates why the Holy Quran refers to people of this type as Jinn or Devils anyone that will not submit to God's Laws. Read Holy Quran Ch 15, Section 3, verse 1336.

Personally speaking, I do not care if the Whiteman is a Devil or not, but it does explain many things that happen on a daily basis, and gives an understanding as to Why the Blackman has been so mis-treated and can't receive Justice from these people. They have the capacity to give Justice if they want to, because the flip side of Evil is Good. I do not recommend that you wait! Your (Blackman) justice lies in doing for yourself! The message has been delivered and we will not get another; you have gotten all the Jesus that you are going to get. THERE IS NO JESUS IN THE SKY. Remember this book is about the "Reality of God and the Devil and how it relates to Black and White People.

Thank you Elijah, for teaching me that Heaven is not in the sky, but rather is a State of Mind! The Blackman must build his own NATION on Earth.

This verse explains it all; Holy Quran, chapter 15, verse 1338 "When a Man is raised to life spiritually, the suggestions and the promptings of the devil cease to affect him. But until he finds spiritual life, evil suggestions mislead him now and then." God and the Devil dwells within the Soul of Man; He must control his devil (evil suggestions) in order to reach the full potential of being God. The Blackman of America can reach his Godly potential by building a "New Nation" for himself with the Divine Guidance of Allah.

The Blackman and Woman of America will build a self-supporting community "nation" in America by applying the "Mental and Spiritual" principle of Evolution, and not by physical Revolution. The revolution that will change the Blackman will be in the Mind! Here are some scriptural references on Aids, and its prevention. There will be a Spiritual Revolution!

How To Avoid Aids in Modern Times!
Lev. 18-22 Unlawful Lust

Thou shall not lie with mankind as with womankind: It is an abomination. 20:13 If a man also lie with Mankind, as he lieth with a Woman, both of them have committed an abomination; they shall surely be put to death; their blood shall be upon them.

Lev. 17:10-11 Blood Transfusion is forbidden

And whatsoever man there is of the House of Israel, or of the strangers that sojourn among you, who eateth any manner of blood (Blood Transfusion) ; I will even set my face against that soul that eateth blood, and will cut him off from among his people. For the life of the flesh is in the blood.

1 Timothy 1:8-10 Drug Addiction is unlawful

8 But we know that the Law is good, if a man use it lawfully. 9 Knowing this, that the law is not made for a righteous man but for the lawless and disobedient, for the ungodly and for the sinners, for unholy and profane, for murderers of fathers, and murderers of mothers, for manslayers, 10 for fornicators, for them that defile themselves

with mankind (Drug Addicts) , and if there be any other thing that is contrary to sound doctrine,

The practicing of God's Words (Scripture) will cure even Aids.

CONCLUSION:
Every Nation (Black People) Must Build on It's Own Birthright; Because That is a Nation's Foundation

The Final War will not be Nuclear, but rather a Race War. Genesis 27:40! To Regain the Blackman's Birthright!

The reason that the Blackman (Lazarus) cannot build an economy for himself is a lack of Unity. The Blackman has been divided morally, family-wise, economically, mentally and spiritually since slavery. This mental division has cause a lack of trust between brothers and sisters and is the basis for not being able to unite on such a vital issue as economical survival. The Blackman trust the whiteman with his life savings and this is the very man that sold him a burial policy that he could only collect, after he was dead. This is the very man that told him to seek his heavenly reward from God after he dies. This is the very man that told him if he got drunk and was unruly that he would go to hell, but yet sold him the whiskey to drank. After all this falsehood and lies, the Blackman has more trust in him than his own kind. THIS IS TRICKNOLOGY!

Rodney King (A Blackman) was brutalized by four white policemen and was tried by twelve white people, in a predominantly white neighborhood in California, the beating episode was video-taped; but yet the white jury found the four white policemen "Not -Guilty" of beating this blackman, and in Detroit, Malice Green was beaten to death by policemen during a traffic incident. White people wanted them (policemen) to go free. These are two of many incidents over the four-hundred years that the Whiteman has been mis-treating the Blackman. The Time has come for something to be done constructively like building our own economy, which also eliminates the thought of being dependent on the Devil for anything. Black must Protect Self.

Unity of the Blackman is all that is required to have Peace and Security from this brutality. Money comes from having your own economy and the means to control your own destiny; May Allah grant us the strength to do what needs to be done. The Blackman must UNITE and stop acting like a child that must have his every need provided for him. IT IS TIME TO STAND UP!

In conclusion of "Stolen Birthright," the Blackman must separate himself mentally and Economically as a people from the lifestyle of whites, and build a society that is economically sound to support their own kind. The motivation for this action may be abuse and mistreatment but the end result is what the blackman needs; Self-sufficiency! The Rodney King incident is only one incident over a period of 437 years with these cold-hearted, insensitive Devils against the blackman. This is Divine separation that will be brought about by God. In reality, Blacks and Whites have nothing to do with it because nature will bring it about.

Truthfully, whites are only doing what comes naturally for them, however, it is unnatural to sit around year after year taken abuse from another race of people. Total Intergration (Mentally, Spiritually, and Economically wherein the Blackman loses his Identity, Economy, Name, and other means to support himself is INSANE ! Separation mentally, spiritually, and physically allows each race to be themselves, with their own name, culture, and identity. WHY DO Black Leadership reject Separation in the proper sense? It is because they have sold out the black community in spirit and accepted the plight of the blackman as a "legal member" of the Whiteman's society. Must there be another Malice Green?

The Blackman is crying out for his own Economy. He is tired of being a vassal or legal entiety in America. Every time something happens, the whiteman enacts some new laws to compensate for the mis-treatment. The Blackman need his own society (Nation of Islam) wherein he can live in peace with his own people and laws of conduct. It is time that the Blackman accept the fact that there are two societies living in America (Black and White) and he must build up his economy so that he can support himself; because the Whiteman has let him know conclusively that, both people (Black an White may live in America, but we don't live in the same world and we never will! Thus build something for yourself like He did! Black and Whites live on the same soil (America) physically, but they live on different planes or gaps that can't be bridged so be satisfied with your own society.

There are many good white people that are working to see that the Blackman receives Justice in American society, often at the expense of bodily harm. These courageous people have sacrificed money, time, and effort to help the Blackman get Justice and God will reward their good works, and it is greatly appreciated. But these are only a few! In 1993, a Blackman still cannot walk in an all-white neighborhood, unless he can prove that he is a porter or caretaker for someone in that neighborhood. That is why it is so obvious that there are two societies with two sets of values in America. (If both societies live by the laws of God then Black and White could exist in peace together).

The slavemaster (White) and slave (Black) relationship has come to a cross-road, and if the whiteman does not repent and change his ways towards the blackman, he will be destroyed by God. This is how it is described in scripture Numbers Chapter 22 verses 26-34 Balaam and his Ass.

26 And the Angel of the Lord further, and stood in a narrow place, where was no way to turn either to the right hand or to the left.
27 And when the ass saw the angel of the Lord, she fell down under Balaam: And Balaam (Whiteman) anger was kindled, and he smote the ass (Blackman) with a staff.
28 And the Lord opened the mouth of the ass (Blackman) and she said unto Balaam (Whiteman) What have I done unto thee, that thy has smitten me these three times?
29 And Balaam said unto the ass, Because thou hast mocked me, I would that there were a sword in my hand, for now would I kill thee.
30 And the ass (Blackman) said unto Balaam (Whiteman), Am not I thine ass, upon which thou hast ridden ever since I was thine unto this day? Was I ever to do so unto thee? And he said, Nay.
31 Then the Lord opened the eyes of Balaam, and he saw the angel of the Lord standing in the way, and his sword drawn in his hand; And he bowed down his head, and fell flat on his face.
32 And the angel of the Lord said unto him, wherefore hast thou smitten thine ass these three times? Behold I went out to withstand thee, and because thy way is preverse before me:
33 And the ass (Blackman) saw me and turned from me these three times: unless she had turned from me (repented), surely now also I had slain thee, and save her alive.
34 And Balaam (Whiteman) said unto the angel of the Lord, I have sinned; for I knew not that thou stoodest

in the way against me. Now therefore, if it displease thee, I will return / to your ways/ again.

And so shall it be in the end of the Resurrection of Black and White; The Blackman will repent of his ways and become the vehicle by which the whiteman sees the error of his ways and repent. If not he will perish as a world-power as a consequence of his deeds.

The Blackman (Slaves of the whiteman's government) will be saved by repenting and looking to God for guidance, and go on to build an ever-lasting kingdom known as the Kingdom of God. The spiritual transition that must take place within the mind of the Negro is this: A negro's mentality is this; A blackman color-wise, but has the Name of the whiteman, has the culture, religion, habits (drinking, eating, sexual, and philosophic outlook on life), hates black, love white, lives from pay-check to pay-check and in general is a mental and spiritual slave to the whiteman. On the other hand, a Blackman (mental and spiritual) has his own black Name, Religion, Culture, Eating habits (no hog), Does not drink poison of any kind (alcohol) love his black-self, respect all people and disrespect no one regardless of race creed or color. Works to build his own economy so that he can support Self and kind. Believe all nations should be self-supporting, and especially the Blackman of America; 437 years in America, first a physical slave, and now a mental and spiritual slave to the Economic System of America. (Blacks are the Children of Israel from Ishmael and Esau's lineage).

The negro must transform his Mind, to the Mind of a Blackman, and God will strengthen his Soul with enough Wisdom, Knowledge, and Understanding to build an economy for himself and his own kind. *It is time scripturally for Genesis 27:40 "KJV" to be fulfilled wherein the Dominion and Yoke is to be broken from the Blackman's neck, thus World-Wide Racial Conflict or WW III.*

The objective of this book was to deliver the Truth; i.e. each nation must live within it's own habitat (land), and live it according to its own destiny, within it's own Mind, and not the Mind of another People!

In conclusion, the Blackman must regain his birthright, of his own volition, it cannot be given back to him by the whiteman. It must be accepted by God and practiced as a normal way of life. A final clarification on God and the Devil. The question is often asked why God made a devil that leads Man astray? God has created Man with two kinds of passions, the higher which awaken in him a spiritual life, and the lower which relate to his physical life; and corresponding to these two passions there are two kinds of beings; the angels (Godly person) and the devils (Evil person). The lower passions become a hindrance to Man in his advancement to a higher life when they are out of control. Man is required to keep his passions under control!

If he can do so, his passions become a help to him in his advancement, instead of a hindrance. The Prophet once said, that Allah has helped him to overcome his (devil); and now his devil (lower passions) has submitted, and now instead of making evil suggestions, it became a help to him in developing his higher life. Allah-U-Akbar! In the final analysis, life itself, is simply God expressing himself through humanity, and Man expressing himself as either an angel or a devil. THIS APPLIES TO ALL PEOPLE, BLACK OR WHITE !

The Last Step

The Blackman of America is ruled by the laws, lifestyle, and power of the Whiteman. He must accept A New Ruler for his Mind; i.e. God and his way of life! This will give him the power to regain his Birthright, develop a new Economy; build a world of his own. This last step is voluntary because God does not force himself on anyone. What was the purpose of this civilization (Whiteman) for the past 6,000 years? To prove than Man must live in Peace with his fellow-man according to the Word of God, because in reality there is only one nation on earth, and that is "The Human Nation." God lives within the Human Family of Man (Not in Sky). God and the Devil is a conceptual term that describes the two-sided nature of Man. It is a spiritual term that indicates the life-style that is most dominant in a person or nation. The Human Nation must learn to live with it's own Self.

The purpose of this book is to show that the Blackman is The Supreme Being of the planet earth, and that he allows certain events to take place in History in order to gain more experience in life; or to prove that he can undergo any experience and come out on top of the situation, thus proving to "HIMSELF" That He Is God, Always Has Been, And Always Will Be! Again, the Blackman Understands the Pattern of Life.

The reason that Jesus Christ is such a central figure in the history of Man is because his life is the pattern of all humans. We (human beings) must be Physically Born, then Spiritually Born, given a life-style or Ministry, Crucified or many trials, Succeed or Fail, and be Resurrected to Heaven (Good Life). The Pattern of Life is: Physical Birth, Spiritual Birth, Ministry, Crucifiction and Resurrection. This is the Blackman's True Birthright; Which cannot be Stolen!

The Blackman's Stolen Birthright is the True Knowledge of God that was stripped from his Mind by a process of "Mental Birth Control." The lack of this knowledge keeps him a mental and spiritual slave in America.

Peace Be Unto You !

REFERENCE:
Correct Meaning of Scriptural Terms !

Heaven and Hell

Heaven and Hell begin in this life. The sustenance that a righteous person receives (Not the fruits and sustenance grown from the earth) are not known or realize by the evil-doers of this world; They are blind to the peace that comes from one's Soul at rest with God and his Laws. When one's Soul is at rest with God, this is the highest spiritual blessing that one can attain in this life. There is no grief, fatigue, or toil, and the heart is purified of all rancour, and jealousy, peace and security reigning all around you; This is Heaven! However, this is not a place for simple enjoyment or rest; it is essentially a place (state of mind) for further advancement to higher and higher stages or states of mind.

Hell is also a state of mind and punishment is not meant for torture but for purification, in order to make person fit for spiritual advancement. The idea underlying hell is; Whoever wasted their opportunity to do good shall, under the inevitable law which makes every man tastes of what he has done be given another chance by under-going a course of treatment (Some people call this a chastisement) for their spiritual diseases, which they have brought about with their own hands. Spiritual diseases are; Lying, Cheating, Stealing, Fornication, Adultery, Murder, Envy, Jealousy and Covetness. It is perfectly clear that when God brings down his punishment it is for our benefit and not to our detriment. In fact, what we are doing is to our detriment and God is trying to save us from our own foolish selves. If it were not for God ordaining a Hell so that we may be saved, we probably would all be dead!

So, Heaven and Hell are two conditions of life for our higher advancement; they become places when we actualize our state of mind to such a degree that we bring into reality. Nothing comes out of the sky except; rain, snow, hail, tornados, or other conditions that come about as a result of a change in atmospheric pressure.

Life After Death

Death is a stage in Evolution. Just as from dust is evolved the man, so it is that from the deeds which he does is evolved the higher man. Death is only a stage in growth. As from the small life germ the man grows up but he does not lose his individuality although he undergoes many changes, so from this man is made the higher man. His attributes changes and he is made to grow into what he cannot conceive at the present. Each stage is a form of death and growing out of that stage is a form of new life. A life after death is normally a new world of advancement, new progress, and the old life becomes insignificant. Physical death settles all things and God did not ordain any physically dead people (including Jesus) to come back and give instructions to live human beings about anything! God uses live people to give instructions to live people. Jesus said it himself "Let the Dead bury the Dead", meaning his message was not for dead people but the living.

The Resurrection is refered to as giving life after death, however it only means a continuation of this present life. A more beautiful life in God, and a complete manifestation of the wicked life that most people are living because of the false concepts that they have accepted as truths; such as Heaven and Hell, The Balance (good and evil), and many others that will be discussed. The Hereafter should be understood, because it does not mean after you die that you will go to heaven or hell, but rather the hereafter means "To be here alive, after the veils have been lifted (falsehoods) from your life and you are raised from a dead state of mind to a heavenly state of mind." All of this can take place in each individual's life time because Heaven and Hell are not two places that you go to but rather are two separate conditions of life. Heaven is a condition that few people know about and that is why so many doubt its' existence for themselves, although most believe there is a Hell and it is a condition of their lives; They are not waiting to go there!

Spiritual Law

God is Law. Gal. 6:7 Be not deceived, God is not mocked, for whatever a man soweth, that shall he also reap. For he that soweth to his flesh, shall of the flesh reap corruption; but he that soweth to the Spirit shall of the Spirit reap life everlasting. When we speak of spiritual law, it has reference to that which pertains to God; A law of God in which he created human beings. Humans think that they can sow corruption and reap blessings; Sow Deceit and reap loyalty; Sow discord and reap peace, however, that is not how the law works. The law of God is that you reap exactly what you have sown. It is the same law as Cause and Effect, in physical science.

Human Beings are created according to law, and not in some helter skelter fashion. That is why man is able to understand the human body because of regularity and consistency in the human being; The human spirit works in the same manner. The law of the human spirit becomes a chain by which man is either bound by good deeds or evil deeds. The rise and fall of Man is due sorely to his ability or inability to live up to the law of his creation;

Which is to do good or perish! God did not intend for man to be evil so he was created in such a way that whatever he does evil to himself or his fellow-man, he would self-destruct. Again; You reap upon yourself that which you sow upon your brother.

When the truth of God comes into the hearts of men who were spiritually dead, they now speak with such power that the whole earth from end to end respond to their call. These men are called Prophets, Mediums or Messengers of God; they were also "spiritually dead" to the knowledge of God at one point in their lives and the transformation was so dramatic that no one could question that God had indeed visited their Soul. The truth is to be obeyed and not rejected!

The Problem

The problem with the world today is a lack of true knowledge about God. Of all the knowledge that one may have or obtain, the Knowledge of God is the greatest and the most necessary of all knowledge. Ninety eight percent of the people of the earth are without the knowledge of God, the Supreme Being. Some facts causing this condition of ignorance are;

1. Looking at the Universe (God's Creation), we wonder, how did God create this universe and himself?

2. His creatures are without numbers and unlimited; how is this?

3. What is true Religion? This world's inability to answer these questions has cause man to worship his own idea or concept of God like spirits, wood, stone, gold, silver, Sun, Moon, and Stars. Some even worship fire, snakes, and water; they worship all the "signs of God" as the real God. This is the real Problem! Not knowing who God is, or how to recognize God in your life.

The Bible tells us who we are and how to recognize God. 1 Cor. 3:16–17. Know ye not that ye are the Temple of God, and that the spirit of God dwelleth in you? If any man defile the Temple of God, him shall God destroy. For the temple of God is Holy, Which temple ye are. Now, the world have become wicked over material goods to the point that they are insane with power. When the world knew God, they glorified him not as God (European Nations) and neither were they thankful, but became vain in their imagination and their foolish hearts were darkened, professing themselves to be wise and they became fools. The world is foolish today for rejecting God's laws and ways of living. They have accepted uncleanliness through the lust of their hearts to dishonor their own bodies between themselves; They have changed the truth of God into a lie, and worship and serve the creature (man) more than the creator. This is the Problem!

Material Civilization

The reason that these modern disasters have been brought on man is because they have become so estranged from God that they can't bear to hear his words. So thoroughly have lust and greed engrossed this world. A portrait of this material civilization that we live in is: "Manufacturing is the number one specialty and pride of the west. "The West is so engrossed in the contest of manufactures that they have no thought of God left in their minds. Production and more production, that is the be-all and end-all of life with them.

Will this great world-conflict bring the world to an end? God is the only one that can restore the balance to the world, human efforts are a complete failure. A revolution will be brought about in the world. This revolution will be a change in the mentality of the nations. Material benefits have turned man into the enemy of man, a spiritual awakening will be brought about which will change the world entirely. Instead of cutting one another's throats, men will learn that they are but one nation. The day of peace for this world will come about when the idea dawns on the mind of man that there is only one nation, the human nation, that lives on this earth.

People that constantly work against the plans of God are brought to disgrace. The meaning is that material acquisitions are fine in and of themselves, but don't neglect your soul or deny others access to God through false teachings like (Jesus is alive in heaven). This is done so that the poor will seek their material reward in heaven (In the Sky), while the rich receive their reward here on earth while they live. It is a type of spiritual mesmerizing of the poor the world-over, and it is this type of awakening to the truth that the poor will receive from God that is called "The Resurrection of the Dead."

All Prophets of God Have Been Called Liars and Rejects !

The true prophets of God suffer much among the disbelievers of the people to whom they are sent until the help of God come to them. Poor Noah, according to the Bible was also a righteous man and was saved from being destroyed by a flood of water intended only for those who had rejected Noah and his warning message of God. They called him a liar and even the Bible charges that Prophet with celebrating his deliverances from the flood with drunkardness. (Gen. 9:21-25), Then, after being sober from wine, he, (Noah) cursed his son, Ham, the father of Canaan just because Ham saw his father's nakedness while he was drunk and told his two brothers about it---which was only natural. Yet, his father desired that he (Ham) be the servant of the other brothers. (Of course, just how true this is I leave it up to you). Yet the Bible does not seem to show anything of a Divine punishment coming to Lot nor Noah for their drunkardness or for Lot getting children by his daughters.

Moses, the great prophet of Jehovah, suffered mockery and envy by his people. Moses, according to the Bible,

(Exodus 6:20) was the son of Amran and his wife Jockebed, his father's sister---which means that Amran, married his aunt, his father's sister. Moses married Zipporah, the daughter of Midian whose name was Jethro. Moses even had trouble with his own wife (Zipporah). She called him a bloody husband to her. She cut the foreskin of her son with a sharp stone and threw it at the feet of Moses, (Exodus 4:25). The Bible charges Moses sister, Miriam and Aaron with speaking against Moses because he had married an Ethiopian woman. She is not the Midian wife, Zipporah (Numbers 12:1). Jehovah punished Miriam with leprosy and Moses had to fast and pray to Jehovah to take this dangerous disease from his sister, although she was at fault. All of the Children of Israel murmured against Moses and Aaron (Numbers 14:2). Moses was a Divine Prophet sent to raise up an evil people to Divine Consciousness, and he was successful in establishing Israel as a Nation. Moses grave has not been found, nor has Moses been seen by the world since his death; nor is he expected to be seen.

David was a man after God in his own heart. But yet this prophet and King is charged with having a woman's husband to hide his act with his wife. He tried in vain to get Uriah (her husband) to stay home and sleep with his wife (Bathsheba) while the Nation was at war. David had him (Uriah) killed and then took the poor man's wife for his own wife. (II Samuel 11:2, 4, 11, 17–27, 12:9). He is also charged with having many wives and hundreds of concubines. According to the Bible (II Samuel 16:21, 22) God returned David's evil to him through his son, Absalom, for the taking of Uriah wife, and having Uriah put to death by putting him on the front line on the battlefield. This son of David, Absalom, went into his father's concubines under a tent on the house-top in the sight of all Israel. "The man who lives in a glass house should not throw stones."

Of all the Saints' and Prophets' deaths, there is more confusion over whether Jesus is dead or living that any man that ever lived on our planet earth. Why? I will show just why. The past Jesus' history of two thousand years ago, was a sign of something to come ! A SIGN OF A NATION BEING BORN UN-NATURAL (Mental Birth) HIDDEN FROM THE WORLD OF IT'S OWN KIND! It refers to the last days of this civilization when God comes to restore the knowledge that has been lost, and reunite the nations of the world unto their own kind. This is known as the "Resurrection of the Dead." The first Jesus was unable to convert the Jews to whom he was sent. On the other hand, the second Jesus will convert the whole world because he will open the eyes of the world to that which has been hidden from them.

The reason that the Bible and the Holy Quran omits what Mary and Jesus were a sign of, was for there own protection, and to serve as a test between the "knowledge of the Believers" and the "knowledge of the Disbelievers" in the last days of this world. There is no record of anyone, regardless to how good or bad they were, coming back to life after being dead and buried, before Jesus nor since Jesus. Just what purpose would Jesus have served two thousand years ago for God to have allowed him to suffer death and bring him back to life, and then hide him from the public's eyes until the end of the world? God never speaks or does a work without a purpose. Again, why should God love Jesus more than any other of his prophets; while Jesus was unable to convert the Jews (to whom he was missioned) to him?

Misunderstandings About Bible

The Bible, King James Version, has been misunderstood, and those misunderstandings are causing confusion the world over. I will attempt to clarify some of them. The time spiritually that we live in is referred to spiritually as the "Resurrection of the Dead." The resurrection of Jesus, from the dead, is now going on the world over, wherein those that were spiritually dead to the Divine knowledge of Self and God, are being risen into it. The first Jesus was born among the spiritually dead Jews and the second Jesus is born into a spiritually dead world that has been poisoned by lies for the past 6,000 years. The difference between the first and second is that the first Jesus failed in his mission to convert the Jews, but the second Jesus will convert the world into righteousness (not instantly, over a period of time) with truth. The Holy Quran says that Jesus said, "When thou didst cause me to die." Jesus (the second) is already in the world today and his spirit is bringing about a gradual change among the Nations of the Earth; gradually, not instantly with truth.

Jesus's Meaning of The Resurrection

Jesus spoke in parables, symbolism and metaphors and one day his disciples said unto him, why speakest thou unto them in parables? Matthew 13:10-11 He answered and said on to them, Because it is given unto you to know the mysteries of the Kingdom of Heaven, but to them it is not given. The hour that Jesus spoke about was the end of the time that this world of evil was given to rule over Mankind; 6,000 years ! The dead that would rise; would be the spiritually dead people that had been killed by falsehood, lies, and misunderstandings, and they would hear the truth and be resurrected spiritually and live. In the last days, all the graves (Nations) shall hear his voice (The second Jesus) and come forth to life or to damnation because of the evil that they have done. The Dead that would rise is the mentally dead negroes of America. Negroes mean Dead.

From an historical perspective (Adam and Eve) to a present or future outlook the subject will refer to Adam and Eve as White People their current identity is all *European Nations* that have spread out all over the planet. Later this global identity will evolve into two distinct separate world powers, and these two powers control the world today! White People or the European Nations have dominated the whole world and thus fulfilled the prophecy of bringing the world into subjection. However at the end of time (1914) the Bible makes it clear that the nation rising up against nation is to the European conflicts that we have witnessed. Basically, White People have subdued the whole world, but could not agree on the division of the spoils, and they are at one another's throats and this struggle has assumed the form of a World War. One world war ends only to be followed by another. We have seen hell raging on this earth in World War II. What World War III may bring, no one can say for sure.

INDEX

A

Abel 36, 160
Abram 1, 2
Abraham 1, 2, 4, 8, 29, 40, 87
Adam 9
Adam and Eve 9, 10, 36, 54
Africa 31, 38, 97
Afro-American 83
Afrocentricity 118
Aids 170, 171
Ali 130
Allah 24, 37, 40, 45, 72, 80, 99
America 30, 31, 34, 39, 49, 52, 59, 61, 81, 102, 131
Angel 24
Animal 11
Apostle 75
Arimathaea 62
Arabic 32, 38
Arabia 34
Arabs 72, 73
Aristotle 124
Asenath 7
Asia 18, 97
Asiactics 31

B

Babies 18, 123
Baker 5
Balaam 175
Beatitudes 56
Beast 11
Beggar 49
Belief 11, 156
Benjamin 7, 8, 14
Bible 13, 19, 23, 31, 64, 73, 99
Birth

Birth Control 38
Birthright 3, 8, 34, 39, 42, 94, 134, 172, 177
Black United Fund 167
Blackman 44, 45, 47, 55, 62, 63, 64, 71, 81, 82, 97, 124, 128
Blacks 9, 31, 32, 38, 92,
Blessed 56
Blessing 3
Blind, 26, 45, 49
Blood 13, 26, 28
Blood Transfusion 170
Born Again 125, 128
Brothers 4, 8

C

Cain 36, 67, 160
Canaan 1, 8
Carpenter 15
Carthage 149
Cat 85
Caucasian 83, 92
Cave 9, 11, 12, 32, 36, 61, 62, 66, 71
Caveman 95
Census 13, 18, 21
Chaldees 1
Cherubin 9
Child 23
Children 2, 8, 16, 20, 147
China 31
Christian 29, 40, 62
Christianity 31, 37, 49, 50, 53, 131, 134, 156, 164
Christ 57
Christ Jesus 15, 28, 42, 54, 99
Christmas 22, 150
Citizen 91
Civil Rights Act 1865 93

189

INDEX

Civil Rights Act 1964 96
Civilization 10, 31, 52, 124
Civil War 138
Clothes 11
Coat 4, 5
Coffin 8
Colonialism 149
Colored 83
Comforter 29, 42
Commandments 57
Constantine Aurelius 149
Crescent 82
Criminals 27
Cross 27, 28
Crucifiction 15, 26, 27
Crusades 72
Cup 6
Culture 112, 126

D

Dan 14
David 21
Dead 23, 24, 30, 32, 40, 41, 48, 51, 55, 135, 156,
Deaf 45, 49
December 15, 22
Delilah 67
Desegregation 94
Deutoronomy 13
Devil 13, 44, 47, 52, 64, 65, 72, 89, 90, 99, 131, 141, 163
Dhu-l-garnain 63
Dietary Laws 85, 92, 153
Disbelief 54
Discrimination 96
Divine 13, 24, 42, 61, 65, 141
Divine Guidance 10, 81
Dog 11, 85
Dominion 8, 9
Dred Scott 91
Dress Code 116
Dumb 45, 49
Drug Addiction 167
Dwellers 61

E

Eagles 106
Ears 6

Earth 9, 31
East 20
Economics 119
Economy 55, 182
Eden 9
Egypt 3, 5, 7, 12, 19, 22
Egyptian 125
Elijah 71
Emerson, John D Dr. 91
Embalmed 8
Embryo frozen 53, 90
England 37, 62
Ephraim 7, 14
Esau 3, 8, 35
Espoused 23
Euphrates 88
Eurocentric 118
Europe 22, 102
European 31, 32, 37, 50, 54, 64, 69, 80, 136
Eve 9
Evil 52
Evolution 51
Ezekiel 102

F

Family 7
Famine 7, 98
Fard 33, 42, 51, 59, 65, 132
Father, 13, 15
Feast 6
Fire 11, 12
Fish 11, 12
Flag 63
Flag of Islam 157
Flesh 28
Fornication 59
Fourteenth Amendment 93
Four Hundred Years 48
Four Thousand Years 102

G

Gad 14
Gabriel 23
Galilee 23, 28
Garden 65
Garden of Eden 9, 10, 143

Garment 5
Genesis 3
Gentiles 35, 38
Germans 31
Germany 37
God 1, 2, 7, 10, 12, 19, 25, 38, 42, 61, 65, 99, 129
God-Consciousness 145
Gog 63, 64, 67, 101
Gold 37
Grafted 85, 92
Grave clothes 49
Grave Mental 47
Great Britain 37
Greed 52
Green, Malice 173

H

Hagar 2
Hair 11
Half-original 125
Hamites 89
Haran 1
Hawkins, John 31, 38
Heaven 28, 50, 53, 73, 144
Hell 50, 144
Hereafter 52
Herodotus 125
Herion 75
Hills 9
hillsides 11
History 102
Hog 92
Holocaust 77
Holy Quran 17, 23
House of Isreal 54, 156
Human Birth Control 92
Human Nation 178
Hypocrites 75

I

Iblis 64, 141
Identity 64, 90
Idolatry 13
Illigetimate 23
Image 12, 166
Immigrants 38

Immortality 65
Indian 37
Interpretation 6
Ishmael 2, 4, 7, 34
Ishmaelites 5
Islam 35, 36, 53, 65, 67, 71, 74
Islam, Nation, 54, 73

J

Jacob 3, 5, 7, 14
Jamacian 81
Jesus 13, 19, 23, 25, 29, 42, 49, 51, 54, 59, 72
Jews 20, 22, 26, 54, 74
Jewish 23, 42
Johnson, Andrew 93
Joseph 4, 6, 15, 16, 18, 62, 87
Juda 14
Judgement Day 24, 141
Jinn 142

K

Kabba 35
Kareem 130
Keys 115
Khadija 35
Kine 6
King of Babylon 103
Kingdom of God 8, 30, 51, 80,
Kingdom of Heaven 57, 145
King James Version 23
King, Rodney 172
Killer 68
Knowledge 13
Kuwait 139

L

Lame 26
Language 165
Law 57
Lazarus 22, 24, 47, 48, 51, 54, 87
Leviticus 13
Life 51
Lies 9
Lincoln, Abraham 93
Lion 73

192 INDEX

Lord 5, 23
Lost People 61
Love 59
Lust 58

M

Magician 6
Magog 63, 64, 67, 101
Man 12, 32, 65, 166
Manasseh 7, 14
Manger 19, 21
Mankind 14, 24, 31, 47
Martha 22, 25, 49
Mary 15, 16, 18, 19, 23, 55
Mecca 34
Mental Birth Control 38, 39, 90
Mentally 25
Mental Sleep 62
Messiah 27
Messenger 61, 71
Middle East 138
Missiouri Compromise 91
Mission 26
Money 30, 63
Moral 60, 63, 154
Moses 9, 10, 12, 15, 29, 37, 57
Muhammad, Ali 133
Muhammad, Ibin A. 29, 33, 37, 61, 71
Muhammad, Elijah 40, 55, 61, 71, 87, 97, 111, 122, 136, 155, 166
Muhammad, Fard 33, 40, 42, 43, 44, 54, 61, 71, 99, 111, 150, 166
Muslim 35, 36, 38, 40, 48, 61, 152

N

Name 4, 153
Naphtoli 14
Nation 2, 40, 169
Nationality 82
Nazareth 23
Nebuchadnezzer 103
Negro 38, 40, 55, 150, 156
Negro, So Called 20, 32, 47, 54, 62, 71, 146
Neighbor 54
Nichodemus 78
Niger River 83
Nigerian 81
Nile River 38
Nimrod 15
Nude 10

O

Original 32
Orthodox 46, 76

P

Palestine 125, 139
Patmos 72
Peace 84
Perjury 59
Pharisees 57
Pharaoh 5, 6, 87
Pig 73
Pilate 28
Polo, Marco 31
Potiphar 5
Prison 5
Precognition 145
Pregnancy 18
Promise Land 111
Prophecy 24, 82
Prophet 2, 13, 17, 35, 54
Prostitution 127

Q

Quran, Holy 17, 18, 21, 34, 61, 63, 71, 99

R

Race 13, 32
Radio-In Head 22
Rat 85
Rebekah 3
Religion 131
Reparation 77
Reuben 14
Revelation 13
Resurrection 15, 23, 24, 25, 26, 29, 40, 41, 46, 52, 63, 73, 100, 150
Reward 27

INDEX

Rich Man 48
Righteousness 57
Rock 141
Rome 150

S

Sabbath 14
Savage 10, 11, 12, 128
Scripture 50, 61, 147
Sea 12
Seed 1, 35, 87
Second Jesus 32, 55
Segregation 93, 94
Self-Image 117, 167
Separate Economics 119–121
Separation 79
Seventh Day 112, 113
Seventh Thousand Year 113
Sex-Theaters 127
Sheaves 4
Ship 31
Simeon 14
Sin 23, 68
Sky 11, 90
Slav 64, 137
Slaves 30, 32, 38, 40, 90, 93, 94
Slavery 39, 93, 98, 130, 136, 159
Slave-Trader 38
Socrates 124
Son 20, 26
Son of Man 45, 101, 161
South Africa 125
Sphinx 37
Spiritual 40, 42
Spiritually 19, 25
Star 4, 63
Stolen Birthright 173, 178
Supreme Being 44, 73, 130

T

Teacher 17
Ten Commandments 22, 145

Telepathy 9, 13
Teutonic 64, 137
Tree 65
Tricknology 172
Truth 9, 71

U

Upright 34
United States 37, 62, 105

V

Vagabond 143
Venison 3
Virgin 23
Viet Nam 138
Voice 12

W

Water 12
Wedlock 19, 132
West Asia 9
Whites 84
Whiteman 44, 46, 50, 62, 63, 95, 131, 169
White People 9, 10, 32, 51, 55
Wife 16
Wilderness 9, 10
Womb 23
Woman, Black 81, 82

X

Malcolm X 133

Y

Yoke 8
Yellow 83
Yusef, Esau IBin 14, 54